Suppose The Wolf Were An Octopus

Grades 5 to 6

A Guide To Creative Questioning For Elementary-Grade Literature

Revised Edition

by
Michael T. Bagley

with new material by
Myrna K. Kemnitz

Royal Fireworks Press

Unionville, New York
Toronto, Ontario

Dedicated to the Memory of
Joyce Paster Foley

Royal Fireworks Press
First Avenue, POB 399
Unionville, NY 10988-0399
(914) 726-4444
FAX: (914) 726-3824
email: rfpress@frontiernet.net

Royal Fireworks Press
78 Biddeford Avenue
Downsview, Ontario
M3H 1K4 Canada
FAX: (416) 633-3010

ISBN: 0-88092-249-4

Printed in the United States of America on acid-free recycled paper using
vegetable-based inks by the Royal Fireworks Printing Company of
Unionville, New York.

Table of Contents

Chapter 1

SPECIFIC PURPOSES OF THE BOOK

1. To demonstrate the procedure for building different levels of questions from children's literature.

2. To encourage teachers to develop questions from all instructional areas.

3. To encourage teachers to use multi-level questions in group discussions.

4. To demonstrate that higher level thinking can be attained through effective questioning.

5. To demonstrate that primary grade literature has the potential to arouse stimulating questions.

6. To provide a number of stories from primary literature, so that a range of subjects and topics are available to teachers.

7. To provide examples of questions at different cognitive levels.

8. To provide several strategies for questioning in the teaching/ learning process.

QUESTIONING IN THE INSTRUCTIONAL PROCESS

"In every age, in every society, there is always one who wonders, one who questions."

Eileen Lynch

Imagination can be enhanced only when one is given the opportunity to play with ideas, to discover relationships, and, most important, to ask questions. If, as educators, we demonstrate to the child that his/her ideas have value and his/her questions will be listened to, we are adding a rich source of fuel to that child's motivation for learning. It seems that involving students in higher level questioning will subsequently lead to a more open-minded, self-confident, inquiring person. It is our contention that teachers who actively engage in asking higher level questions will stimulate and increase the amount of child-initiated questions with teachers, family and peers.

Hypothesis No. 1

Teachers who show an appreciation for questioning, who establish a climate where diverse questions are valued, who consistently ask high quality questions will develop students who demonstrate greater involvement in the questioning process.

Students who are encouraged to ask questions are being given an opportunity to explore with their minds, to gain meaning for themselves and to relate new data with old concepts. The new questions, new theories and new ideas remain the most important part of the learning process.

Another benefit in using higher level questions is that it can provide an open-ended learning situation. When one seeks to ask questions about things or events that have no one right answer or a multitude of potentially right answers, an attitude develops where one appreciates the immensity and complexity of the real world data. Perhaps this point can be illustrated by the following quotation:

"Just when I knew all of life's answers, they changed all the questions."

Hallmark Card, Inc.

It is our belief that a classroom situation where questioning is held in high regard will result in an environment that is healthier, and one in which students are more receptive.

Hypothesis No. 2

Teachers who use higher level questions on a consistent basis will increase their students' higher level thinking skills in terms of frequency, depth, appropriateness and complexity.

This second hypothesis involves a concept which is paramount to our beliefs and practices. It is a relationship between good question asking and diverse thinking experiences. One of the basic goals in education is to provide opportunities which will stimulate the learners' higher level thinking skills. A method conducive to enhancing the students' thinking skills is an inquiry-based approach to learning.

QUESTIONING. . . THE BASIS OF INQUIRY

Inquiry is defined by J. Richard Suchman (1968) as a fundamental and natural process of learning by which an individual gathers information, raises and tests hypotheses, builds theories, and tests them empirically. If we relate questioning to this definition, several points can be made.

First, we feel that questioning is a natural process fueled by curiosity—a basic human characteristic. Second, in order to collect data, we must ask questions about the different sources, types and significance of that data. Third, when one begins to develop his/her own theories, we can assume that this person went through the process of question-asking; and, finally, one of the basic findings or conclusions usually generated from rigorous investigation is the development of new, unanswered questions.

If we believe that inquiry is a necessary condition for independence and autonomy of learning, then we must give serious attention to the role of questioning in the teaching/learning process.

We have taken Suchman's three concepts and related them to the questioning process.

Freedom

The more rules and restrictions thrown in the way of the child, the less chance he/she has for asking questions or responding to the questions of others. A part of freedom is autonomy and an autonomous learner will undoubtedly question.

Responsiveness

The child who questions must have a rich supply of data available when he or she wants it. Children who question freely and have access to a responsive statement are bound to come up with formulations that represent the way that child sees and attempts to account for the phenomena of his/her world.

Focus

Questioning is most productive when it has direction and purpose. It is the teacher's role to guide and assist the learner in focusing on relevant topics and issues, or as Suchman emphasizes, "discrepant events." These are events that present a phenomena that does not coincide with the child's knowledge and understanding of the world. A gap is created between what the child perceives and what he/she knows.

It is the teacher's responsibility to maintain the conditions of freedom, responsiveness and focus.

THE CLIMATE FOR QUESTIONING

In order for questioning to take place, the climate of the classroom must be conducive. This climate does not happen by accident, and creating it requires a conscious effort on the part of the teacher. A classroom that is full of excitement, a sense of wonder, and an openness to ideas, where there is thoughful consideration of data, a willingness to take risks, and a lack of concern over personal achievement—this is where questioning will take place. A classroom characterized by an authoritative text and an equally authoritarian teacher stifles questioning.

The teacher can shape the classroom climate. If he/she provides psychological space for students to ask divergent questions without fear of failure or embarrassment, the proper climate is likely to develop.

A climate that encourages students to think and question beyond the scope of the curriculum will yield greater student productivity and a more exciting learning environment. In recognizing the importance of establishing a climate which rewards divergent thinking, Torrance, P. (1963) suggests that teachers respond to students in the following ways: a) Treat unusual questions with respect; b) Treat unusual ideas with respect; b) Provide opportunities for self-initiated learning; d) Show children that their ideas have value; e) Provide periods of non-evaluative practice or learning.

Students who are exposed to this type of learning environment will gain confidence in themselves as autonomous learners. If the teacher is always didactic and restrictive or if he/she plays the role of the ultimate authority in the classroom, the students will develop a dependency on the teacher in an effort to play his/her game and receive the rewards offered.

Reason can answer questions, but imagination has to ask them!

Ralph W. Gerard

BLOOM'S TAXONOMY OF EDUCATIONAL OBJECTIVES

The basic framework for this text comes from the work of Benjamin Bloom (1956), who created the classification of educational objectives in a book called *Taxonomy of Educational Objectives*. In his book, Bloom presents six major cognitive operations: Knowledge, Comprehension, Application, Analysis, Synthesis, and Evaluation. In order to better understand these constructs, we have presented a brief description below of each classification.

Level	Description
L-1 Knowledge	These are questions that check the basic facts about people, places or things (information gathering).
L-2 Comprehension	These are questions that check your understanding and memory of facts (confirming).
L-3 Application	Application questions test your ability to use your knowledge in a problem-solving, practical manner (illuminating).
L-4 Analysis	These are questions in which we select, examine and break apart information into its smaller, separate parts (breaking down).
L-5 Synthesis	Synthesis questions are those in which you utulize the basic information in a new, original or unique way (creating).

L-6 Evaluation   These are questions which help us decide on the value of our information. They enable us to make judgements about the information (predicting).

According to Bloom (1956), the major purpose for constructing the taxonomy of educational objectives was to facilitate communication. It was conceived of as a method for improving the exchange of ideas and materials among test workers, as well as other people concerned with educational research and curriculum development. A more detailed description of the levels and skills can be found in Appendix 1.

Most educators will agree that the upper four levels of the taxonomy, Application, Analysis, Synthesis and Evaluation represent the so-called higher thinking processes. Questions that contain the elements or processes of these taxonomy levels are designed to engage the learner in behavior which requires a more abstract, sophisticated integration of content and experience. There is a complexity of thinking generated at these levels which is not found at the lower levels of the taxonomy, Knowledge and Comprehension. The higher level questions require the student, a) to concentrate and observe details; b) to relate past experience with new data for the purpose of creating unique relationships, and c) to judge the validity of this new information which might be used in predicting future events.

We have often heard that process is more important than fact (or product) and that, as teachers, we must consistently facilitate process learning in our classrooms, regardless of the proliferation of materials designed for the Knowledge and Comprehension thinking levels. To provide an equalizer for the preponderance of lower level curriculum experiences, one must carefully develop material, and arrange encounters for the learner that will stimulate and support higher level thinking processes.

In addition to using children's literature for good questioning, we suggest teachers consider using these practices in all areas of instruction. Good questioning can be used effectively in the following learning experiences:

Category	Description
1. Demonstrations	In demonstrating a new skill or learning activity, the teacher may ask students questions to facilitate meaning.
2. Discussions	General discussions about current event topics offer teachers an excellent opportunity to get students to think.
3. Multi-Media Presentations	Media can create a stimulating encounter for young children. The teacher can ask the students either general type questions or questions specifically related to an event or situation viewed by the class.
4. Field Trips	The effectiveness of a particular field trip relates to the ability of the teacher to raise certain questions. These questions will enable students to integrate previous meanings with the field trip experience.

5. Debates/Role Playing	These activities have great potential for involving students in questioning. They are self-directed, student initiated and highly motivating.
6. Independent Study	The teacher can monitor a student's progress in an independent study through questioning. This provides the student and teacher with an opportunity to analyze the knowledge gained and the direction the student is taking.

Questions are the creative acts of intelligence.

Frank Kingdon

While these activities are conducive for good questioning, not all questions are planned. A teacher who practices good questioning in all aspects of the curriculum will undoubtedly use questioning in a spontaneous natural way. Once the proper climate has been established, teachers and students will engage freely and openly in spontaneous questioning. This may lead to further inquiry by the students. It is our contention that thinking skills at a qualitative level can be enhanced through effective and appropriately-timed questions and discussion sessions.

According to Dorothy Sisk (1974), teachers need to become more aware that synthesizing, summarizing, and concluding can be done quite adequately by the students. Allowing students these opportunities will increase the likelihood that they will experience learning at a higher process level. If a teacher always has the concluding statement, the student realizes that this skill is one he/she need not develop.

How Can the Taxonomy of Questions Help Teachers?

Students frequently do not develop skills in using or creating ideas because they have insufficient opportunities to practice these forms of thought.

Morris M. Sanders

The following guide has been prepared by Sisk, D. (1974), for the purpose of helping teachers pose multi-level questions:

Question Guide

Purpose	Question
To build vocabulary	Do any of you know another meaning of the word "levity" as it was used to describe this situation?
To encourage interpretive thinking	Here we have further information and data; do you have any new ideas or hypotheses?
To encourage planning	How might we go about testing this idea?
To encourage predicting	What do you think will happen when Caliban sees Miranda?
To encourage creative thinking	How might we go about solving this predicament in another fashion?

The taxonomy of questions offers teachers several interesting possibilities relating to the teaching/learning. These possibilities will be presented in random order, considering individual differences have a significant influence on the usability and success of a particular approach to questioning. The following are strategies which integrate the taxonomy with various curricular components:

STRATEGY 1: *Selection of Instructional Material*

The taxonomy could be used as criteria for determining the appropriateness of specific content. Is the material aimed at a specific level of thinking and, if so, at what level and complexity?

STRATEGY 2: *Building Curriculum*

As one plans differentiated learning activities for students, it might be helpful to use the various skills, e.g., verbs, related to particular thinking levels. Kaplan, S. (1974) lists numerous verbs for curriculum development. Appendix 11, Clark, B. (1979) presents an interesting model called the Taxonomy Circle, which is a good technique. Included in the circle are the taxonomy levels, suggested activities, and possible products to be developed.

STRATEGY 3: *Building Questions From Reading Material*

In developing the questions in this text, we used both the taxonomy and verb delineations. It was helpful to have had several models and descriptions of the taxonomy while preparing the questions.

STRATEGY 4:   *Independent Study*

One of the major points in support of independent study is that higher level thinking skills are experienced by the learner in a natural, reality-based way. The teacher could analyze the student's activities using taxonomy as criterion.

STRATEGY 5:   *Student Selected Activities*

Providing students with decision-making opportunities is crucial to the educational process. We have seen one teacher use the taxonomy in the following manner: Students were asked to select from column one a theme, issue or problem. Next, they had to select a process from an extensive list of verbs associated with the taxonomy. Finally, they had to select a means for displaying their project, i.e., products. While this may seem highly structured, it does allow for student decision making, and it familiarizes the students with the process' terminology.

STRATEGY 6:   *Analyze Student Initiated Verbal Interactions*

In group discussion activities, you may want to evaluate the quality and type of questions being initiated by certain students. Newton, F. (1970), has demonstrated that certain behaviors of an inquirer can be accurately observed and classified. Then we might consider using the taxonomy as a means of measuring student verbal interactions at different intervals during the school year.

The strategies listed above represent several possible uses for the taxonomy. We recognize that the use of these strategies will vary among different teaching styles. However, the taxonomy does provide some structure and organization to the curriculum process. If used appropriately (not in isolation) it can be advantageous to the teacher and student.

In exploring the uses of the Taxonomy of Objectives, Sanders, N. (1966), suggests three hypotheses:

1. Students who have more practice with intellectual skills will develop them to a greater degree than those who have less practice.

2. After a teacher studies the taxonomy, he/she is likely to offer students a greater variety of intellectual experiences than he/she did before.

3. A greater emphasis on the teaching of the intellectual skills (other than the memory level) will not decrease the amount of knowledge the student retains.

Three factors are presented by Sanders, N. (1966), which reflect the kind of thinking that is brought about in the minds of students by any questions: First, the nature of the questions. Second, one must be aware of the knowledge of the subject that each student brings to the classroom. The third factor that enters into the classification of a question concerns the instruction that precedes the asking of a question.

For the most part, teachers can anticipate the amount of knowledge students have on a subject and the mental process they will use to arrive at an answer.

The following points are offered by Carin, A., and Sund, R., (1978) concerning a questioning classroom environment:

1. The development of human talent and a positive self-concept hinges on the ability of the teacher to ask stimulating questions. This is basic to student-centered instruction.

2. The classification of questions assists instructors in determining how well they are teaching at the higher levels of instruction.

3. Proper questioning is a sophisticated art of teaching.

4. Higher level questions may be planned before class or spontaneously created through student interaction.

5. Fundamental to improving questioning techniques and formulating superior questions is the necessity of proper classification.

6. Research indicates that teachers specifically trained to ask better questions improve significantly in constructing and using them in the classroom. They become more adept at stimulating human potential.

7. Teachers who increase their wait-time in classroom discussions are likely to get more creative, productive thinking, longer and better responses, and a better quality of student-initiated questions. (Appendix III, *What Happens to Students When Longer Wait-Times Occur?*)

Teachers who maintain classroom environments in which students have freedom to ask questions, to theorize, and to respond to the questions raised by others will observe optimal changes in student behavior. These behavioral changes are described by the following student actions:

1. Asks a series of questions related to the one variable within the problem.

2. Sharpens a subsequent message to fine clarity after having had teacher seek clarity on previous occasions.

3. Asks to be allowed to get "his own answer."

4. Goes to data source spontaneously.

5. Follows the statement of a theory with a data probe to test it.

6. Shares a cause (theory) and doesn't ask the teacher to confirm it.

7. Shares an inference that coincides with data he/she has generated.

Some of these student actions may seem difficult to observe in any ordinary classroom. However, as one begins to concentrate on the effects of a questioning environment, one develops a proficiency at observing specific behaviors, such as the ones listed above. It is rewarding to observe these changes in student behavior, after having created an appropriate climate and practiced good questioning strategies.

THE ROLE OF THE TEACHER IN QUESTIONING

1. It is not the intention of the writers to present these stories in any particular sequence. All questions need not be used for each story. If desired, questions from certain taxonomy levels may be omitted.

2. The language presented in the questions may be refined or adjusted to meet the needs of the individual children.

3. We encourage teachers to develop their own questions for other stories they wish to read to the class.

4. Advanced students should be encouraged to develop questions using the taxonomy levels.

5. The questions may be presented to the entire class or to small groups.

6. We encourage teachers to practice longer wait-time when initiating questions.

7. In monitoring and evaluating the types and levels of questions, we recommend the use of a tape recorder. This procedure can be used periodically to analyze discussion periods where questioning is the focus of the learning encounter.

8. Listen to discussion periods in other classrooms. Compare your questioning techniques with the techniques of other staff members.

9. Discuss the different types and levels of questions with the students. Encourage them to use the appropriate terminology and/or classification system while they are involved in discussion groups or when they are inquiring about certain data.

Kipton and Gruff
Book One of The Kipton Chronicles

by Charles L. Fontenay

Fourteen-year-old Kipton lives on Mars in the first Earth-colony quietly enough until her Uncle Charlie is killed almost before her eyes. Refusing to accept the adults' decision that it was suicide, she investigates. Uncle Charlie had just returned from a surface expedition, and he might have been erased because of his discovery. Gruff, her stuffed bear, is Kipton's alter-ego side kick.

LEVEL 1 (KNOWLEDGE)

o What planet is The Pile on?

o Who is Kipton?

o Who is Gruff?

o What countries from Earth are involved in scientific research on Mars?

LEVEL 2 (COMPREHENSION)

o Describe The Pile.

o Tell what research the scientific corporations are conducting.

o Explain how Kipton communicates with Gruff.

o Describe Kipton's whereabouts at the scene of the crime.

LEVEL 3 (APPLICATION)

o Why are people so interested in going to Mars?

o Would you consider living in an Earth-colony on Mars? Explain.

o Will an Earth-colony on Mars be possible during your lifetime?

o Would Kipton make a good friend? Explain.

LEVEL 4 (ANALYSIS)

o How is living in The Pile like living in a city on Earth? How is it different?

o Why is Kipton so sure Uncle Charlie was murdered?

o How does Kipton's experience with ciphers help to solve the crime?

o Analyze the repercussions of Uncle Charlie's discovery.

o If the planet were terraformed, what would happen to Martian life forms?

o Why does Jack want to help Kipton?

LEVEL 5 (SYNTHESIS)

o Tell how conversing with an alter-ego can help you.

o Describe where Gruff lives. What does he eat?

o What kind of mysteries do you think Kipton and Gruff will solve in future stories in the series?

o Suppose Kipton had a brother or sister. How would that change the story?

o Tell how marsrambler transportation could benefit some areas on Earth.

o Why does Kipton dream of Gruff in an Earthly landscape?

LEVEL 6 (EVALUATION)

o Should there be an Earth-colony on Mars?

o What aspects of human nature will be the most difficult to deal with?

o Should Mars be terraformed. Why?

o Will Kipton make a good girl detective? Explain.

o Is the society of The Pile possible? How far in the future is it?

o What makes this series a real classic for the 21st Century?

Are You There God? It's Me, Margaret

by Judy Blume

Margaret Simon, almost twelve, chats with God a lot. Don't let New Jersey be too horrible (she's just moved from New York to the suburbs). I just told my mother I wanted a bra. Please help me grow God. You know where. Throughout the story, Margaret asks God to help her mature.

LEVEL 1 (KNOWLEDGE)

○ Who was Margaret's best friend?

○ To whom did Margaret write letters?

○ What was the name of the boy Margaret put in her Boy Book?

○ What was the name of the girls' special club?

LEVEL 2 (COMPREHENSION)

○ Describe Margaret's special project for Mr. Benedict.

○ Describe the games the boys and girls played at Norman Fishbein's party.

○ Explain why Margaret and her friends wanted to grow up.

○ Describe Margaret's religious experiences.

LEVEL 3 (APPLICATION)

○ Do you know who is like Margaret? Explain

○ Would you like to be a member in the girls' special club? Why?

○ Have you ever tried to talk to God?

o When and for what reason have you tried to talk to God?

LEVEL 4 (ANALYSIS)

o Analyze the concerns the girls had about life. What would you say about them?

o Why did Margaret have such difficulty with religion?

o How normal were the girls' concerns about nature?

o Which event in the story did you find most amazing?

o Compare Margaret to a sixth grade girl you know.

o Why is this story such a real account of the lives of young people?

LEVEL 5 (SYNTHESIS)

o Suppose you were Margaret's younger brother or sister. What would you say to her if you knew about her talks with God?

o Tell what Margaret would like about your school.

o Think of a name for a club that you'd like to form.

o Describe what life will be like for Margaret and her friends in seventh grade.

o Suppose God answered Margaret back. What would God have said to her?

o Think of what Margaret will ask God in the future.

LEVEL 6 (EVALUATION)

o Why did Margaret feel frustration about her age and development?

○ Judge whether Margaret's private conversations with God were typical of young people.

○ Judge which conversations with God were unreasonable.

○ What would Margaret's parents have said to her concerning all her conversations with God?

○ Predict whether Margaret will continue her conversations with God in the future.

○ What did you learn from this story? Be specific.

Then Again, Maybe I Won't

by Judy Blume

Tony Miglione is a thirteen year old who is fascinated by his best friend's sister, Lisa. He dreams of Lisa and gets embarrassed by his constant thinking of her. A well rounded kid, Tony experiences all the challenges facing a thirteen year old. A realistic, honest, compassionate story of a "real boy."

LEVEL 1 (KNOWLEDGE)

○ Where did Tony and his family move to?

○ Who became Tony's best friend?

○ What did Joel do that really disturbed Tony?

○ Over whom did Tony have a fascination?

LEVEL 2 (COMPREHENSION)

○ Describe why leaving Jersey City was difficult for Tony.

○ Describe the kinds of activities Tony got involved in after he moved to Queens.

○ Why was Tony so attracted to Lisa?

○ Tell what Tony's thoughts were toward the end of the story.

LEVEL 3 (APPLICATION)

○ Have you ever had to move to a new location? Tell what it was like.

○ Have you ever known anyone to steal as Joel did?

○ Do thirteen-year-old boys have frequent dreams about girls? Explain.

○ Can you describe one of your dreams about the opposite sex?

LEVEL 4 (ANALYSIS)

○ How is Tony like an average thirteen-year old?

○ Compare Tony to a thirteen-year-old boy you know.

○ Why was Tony more interested in Lisa than Corky who was more his age?

○ Analyze why Tony had stomach problems.

○ Why did Tony begin to laugh at his experiences toward the end of the story?

○ Compare this story to the one of Judy Blume's stories for younger children.

LEVEL 5 (SYNTHESIS)

○ Suppose Lisa knew how often Tony thinks of her. What would she say to him?

○ Suppose Tony was caught shoplifting with Joel. How would Tony's parents have reacted?

○ Think of another embarrassing situation Tony may get himself into in the story.

○ Suppose Tony won a lottery worth $1,000,000. How would he have spent it in his new home in Queens?

○ What other things did Tony dream about other than Lisa?

○ What if Tony had moved to California or Florida where the climate is warm most of the year? How would he have adjusted to this area? Explain.

LEVEL 6 (EVALUATION)

○ Judge Joel's character.

○ Is it normal to dream the way Tony did? Explain.

○ What might happen to someone caught shoplifting?

○ Who do you think is more clever? Tony or Joel? Why?

○ Predict what kind of person Tony will be when he grows up.

○ What did you learn from this story? Explain.

The Dragon Charmer

by Ruth Siburt

The year is 2080 and thirteen-year-old Elizabeth becomes a secret dragon charmer. He futuristic world is a foreboding place. As she reads through the magical reference book about dragons, she discovers that her father, whom she thought dead, is alive and active doing good deeds. While caring for the little dragon, she sets out to find out what happened to her father.

LEVEL 1 (KNOWLEDGE)

o When does this story take place?

o What is the job of a dragon charmer?

o How does a librarian change Elizabeth's life?

o What is Rad-scan?

LEVEL 2 (COMPREHENSION)

o Describe how dragons grow and get their scales.

o Explain how Elizabeth got to be the new dragon charmer.

o Tell about Elizabeth's school.

o Explain why Rad-scan was used.

LEVEL 3 (APPLICATION)

o Why would you like to be a dragon charmer?

o Have you ever wondered what public health agencies do? What do they do?

o Would you accept Elizabeth as a friend, or would you consider her too dangerous to be around?

o If you didn't use Rad-scan, would you have told Elizabeth?

LEVEL 4 (ANALYSIS)

o Why does the author limit the music in the book to Elizabeth's mother's singing and the dragon's song?

o Compare Elizabeth's personality to her sister's personality.

o Which event in the story do you think is the most important?

o Compare Elizabeth to someone you know who is a risk taker.

o Why did the government allow Rad-scan to be used?

o Analyze Elizabeth's father's reasons for not telling his family that he was really alive.

LEVEL 5 (SYNTHESIS)

o Create another action sequence that Elizabeth's father might have been involved in.

o How would your parents react to you being a dragon charmer?

o If you were taught by group interactive television, how would you behave?

o Describe what the dragon looked like at the end of the story. Be specific.

o Give the story a new title.

o Make up another close call for Elizabeth to have at school concerning the dragon's discovery.

LEVEL 6 (EVALUATION)

o Should children be responsible for their actions?

o Why could Elizabeth's sister hear the dragon?

o How did biblio-vox system audio books further control people?

o What could have happened to Elizabeth, legally, if the dragon did not help her?

o Predict what would have happened to humanity if Elizabeth's father had not had the courage to take action.

o How would you rate Elizabeth's ability as a dragon charmer?

The Incredible Journey
A Tale Of Three Animals

by Sheila Burnford

An incredible journey made by three animals, an old English bull terrier, a large red-gold Labrador retriever, and a Siamese cat. Their journey, which lasted several weeks, took them through the Canadian wilderness. The difficult encounters with nature and other animals is vividly described day by day.

LEVEL 1 (KNOWLEDGE)

○ What were the three animals that made the incredible journey?

○ Where did the animals live?

○ With whom did the bull terrier have a vicious fight during the journey?

○ What happened to the Siamese cat during the journey?

○ Which animal was seen first when they were finally found?

LEVEL 2 (COMPREHENSION)

○ Describe the difficulties the old bull terrier encountered.

○ Explain what the animals had for food during their journey.

○ Tell how the Siamese cat died during the journey.

○ Explain how the animals were found by Mr. Longridge.

LEVEL 3 (APPLICATION)

○ Have you ever had a pet run away? Explain.

○ Would a pet dog or cat that you know make such an incredible journey?

○ Would the three animals in the story have been able to make a similar journey in the area where you live? Explain.

LEVEL 4 (ANALYSIS)

○ Which animal in the story was most responsible for the success of the journey?

○ Which event in the story was the most threatening for the animals?

○ Why didn't the animals return shortly after starting the journey?

○ Where did the animals learn how to kill other animals for food?

○ Which event in the story made you feel the saddest?

○ Which animal had the greatest chance for surviving such a journey? Why?

LEVEL 5 (SYNTHESIS)

○ Name other dangerous situations the animals might have encountered.

○ Suppose one of the animals was killed at the outset. How would that have changed the journey?

○ Name other animals the bull terrier, Labrador retriever and Siamese cat might have seen during the journey.

○ If you had found the three animals, what would you have done?

○ Change the ending to the story. Have the journey continue.

○ Describe the journey from the point-of-view of the Siamese cat.

LEVEL 6 (EVALUATION)

○ Is it possible that these three animals could have made such a journey? Why?

○ What was the most difficult aspect of the journey?

○ Evaluate the search efforts to locate the animals.

○ Judge whether these animals would have protected one another during a real journey.

○ Predict whether any of the animals will attempt such a journey again.

○ To which pet would you give the "most valuable animal award?" Why?

The Summer Of The Swans

by Betsy Byars

A young girl named Sara gains confidence and a better feeling of self after locating her younger brother, Charlie, who had been missing for a day.

LEVEL 1 (KNOWLEDGE)

○ What was Sara's sister's name?

○ What did Sara take Charlie to see?

○ Where was Charlie found?

○ Who called Sara on the phone after Charlie had been found?

LEVEL 2 (COMPREHENSION)

○ Describe Sara's attitude about life.

○ Explain what Sara complained about.

○ Describe how Charlie became lost.

○ Tell how Charlie was found.

LEVEL 3 (APPLICATION)

○ Do you know anyone who has a low self-image? Explain

○ Do you know anyone who has a handicapped brother or sister? Explain their situation.

○ If your brother had gotten lost, describe how you would feel.

○ What did you learn from this story? Explain.

LEVEL 4 (ANALYSIS)

○ Why did Sara find life difficult at times?

○ Compare Sara with her sister.

○ Which event in the story gave you the impression of how negative Sara was?

○ What type of person was Aunt Willie?

○ Why did Sara have a change in attitude after finding Charlie?

○ Analyze Sara's feelings toward her brother Charlie.

LEVEL 5 (SYNTHESIS)

○ What other events or situations could have created a change in Sara's attitude?

○ What would you have said to Sara during the early part of the story about her negative attitude?

○ How else could Charlie have gotten lost?

○ How else could they have located Charlie after he was missing?

○ How does having a brother like Charlie give you strength?

○ Create a "moral" to the story.

LEVEL 6 (EVALUATION)

○ Judge why Sara had such a negative attitude.

○ Judge the type of mother Aunt Willie was.

○ What will the family do to prevent Charlie from getting lost again?

○ How do thoughts affect our behavior? Explain.

○ Predict what Sara's attitude will be like in the future.

○ What three things does this story teach you?

The Adventures Of Tom Sawyer

by Mark Twain (Samuel L. Clemens)

A marvelous story about the curiosity and challenges of a boy's quest to explore nature and life: his friendships, his dangers, his rewards, and his unique personal qualities—all of which makes this story a must for all young readers!

LEVEL 1 (KNOWLEDGE)

○ Who was Tom Sawyer's guardian?

○ Where did young Tom Sawyer live?

○ Who were Tom's best friends?

○ What did Tom and his good friend Huck discover?

LEVEL 2 (COMPREHENSION)

○ Describe what Tom and Huck witnessed while visiting the graveyard one night.

○ Tell about Tom's experience living on the island with Huck and Joe.

○ Explain how Tom and Becky almost died.

○ Tell how Tom became wealthy.

LEVEL 3 (APPLICATION)

○ Which part of Tom's life interests you the most? Why?

○ Why would you have liked to have been Tom Sawyer? Explain.

○ Tell how Tom Sawyer would react to living in your neighborhood.

○ How would you have gotten along with Tom had you lived in St. Petersburg?

LEVEL 4 (ANALYSIS)

○ Why was Tom Sawyer such an exciting individual?

○ What did Tom enjoy doing the most? Explain.

○ Which event in the story demonstrated the lifestyle present in Tom Sawyer's day?

○ Compare Tom Sawyer and Huck Finn.

○ Name the events in the story which could have ended Tom's life.

○ Compare Tom's adventures to the adventures of someone his age living in your community.

LEVEL 5 (SYNTHESIS)

○ Think of some other adventures that Tom and Huck would love to get involved in.

○ Which popular sport would Tom Sawyer do well in? Why?

○ If Tom and his friends had a club, what would they have named it?

○ Suppose you could spend a half-hour with Tom Sawyer. What would you like to talk about? Why?

○ Name three places in the world Tom Sawyer would love to visit? Why?

○ Suppose Tom's mother and father were alive. How would that have changed his adventures?

LEVEL 6 (EVALUATION)

○ Why was Tom Sawyer such an exciting individual?

○ Evaluate the type of events and situations Tom would look for in his young life.

○ Judge the relationship Tom had with Huck Finn.

○ Based on the story, do you think Tom will marry Becky? Why?

○ What would Tom Sawyer's grades be like on today's traditional report card?

○ Give three reasons why the adventures of Tom Sawyer will always be a classic.

Harly Weaver and the Race Across America

by Ken Mays

Twelve-year-old Harly has a dream to compete in the bicycle Race Across America. He trains mentally and physically and races as an unofficial entry.

LEVEL 1 (KNOWLEDGE)

o How old is Harly?

o What is his dream?

o What are the duties of a support team?

o Make a list of a bike's parts.

LEVEL 2 (COMPREHENSION)

o Describe why the newspaper owner was eager to do Harly's story.

o Why did Harly's muscles begin to hurt during practice?

o Describe the change that came over his older sister.

o Describe the affects of a strict regimen on Harly's social and school life.

LEVEL 3 (APPLICATION)

o Why do athletes follow very specific diets? Do you? Explain.

o Have you read about or seen on TV news about the famous Tour de France bike race? Tell about it.

o If you ride a bicycle, how far do you ride before you feel fatigued.

o Is Harly's bike like your bike? Explain.

LEVEL 4 (ANALYSIS)

o Why was it necessary for Harly to have a sponsor?

o Why did merchants get on Harly's bandwagon?

o Analyze Harly's method of training for the big race.

o Explain how Harly's physical growth affects the fine tuning of the bike.

o Analyze the emotional strain on Harly during the race.

o Compare the physical strain on Harly during his practice sessions to the strain during the actual race.

LEVEL 5 (SYNTHESIS)

o What would have happened if Harly's bike could not be adjusted to his new size?

o How would the story change if Harly's mother had not perceived herself as part of his positive effort?

o What would have changed if Harly had dreamed of becoming a marathon runner?

o Create a home page web site for a cyclist chat group.

o Suppose Harly was a girl. How would the story change?

o Think of a good human interest headline for an article about Harly.

LEVEL 6 (EVALUATION)

o What kind of responsibility does making a dream come true carry with it?

o How would Harly have reacted if his family forbade him from cross-country racing?

o Predict how Harly's classmates and teachers will treat him from now on.

o What makes this story a real life experience?

o Predict if Harly will enter the Race Across America when he is eligible.

o In what way was Harly a winner even though he dropped out of the race?

Danny, The Champion Of The World

by Roald Dahl

The story is a terrific adventure story—about a boy, his dad, and a daring and hilarious pheasant-snatching expedition. And, just as important, it's the story of the relationship between a boy and his father who, in Danny's own words, "without the slightest doubt, was the most marvelous and exciting father any boy ever had."

LEVEL 1 (KNOWLEDGE)

○ Where did Danny live?

○ Where did the pheasants live?

○ What did Danny and his father give to the pheasants which led to their capturing the birds?

○ How old was Danny when he drove his father's car?

LEVEL 2 (COMPREHENSION)

○ Describe where Danny lived with his father.

○ Explain what happened to Danny's father one night during a pheasant hunt.

○ Describe two secret methods Danny's father used to capture pheasants.

○ Tell how Danny and his father captured more than a hundred pheasants.

LEVEL 3 (APPLICATION)

○ Do you know a hunter? Describe this person. What does s/he like to hunt?

o Could you have driven your dad's car at age nine—as Danny did in the story? Explain.

o Where do people hunt pheasants in your part of the country?

o Can you think of some tricks hunters use to capture pheasants?

LEVEL 4 (ANALYSIS)

o What type of person was Danny's dad? Explain.

o Which event in the story really scared you? Describe it.

o Compare Danny's life to the way you live.

o Analyze what might have happened to Danny when he went looking for his dad.

o Why would you have liked to have been Danny in the story? Explain.

o Compare Mr. Victor Hazell with Danny's father.

LEVEL 5 (SYNTHESIS)

o Suppose Danny had a few brothers or sisters. How might that have changed the story?

o What if Danny and his father were caught by Mr. Hazell during their great hunt?

o Name some animals Danny and his father might like to hunt.

o Think of other ways Danny and his father could have captured so many pheasants.

o If Danny lived in your neighborhood, what kinds of things would he want to do?

o Make up a new title for this adventure story.

LEVEL 6 (EVALUATION)

○ Judge the secret methods Danny's father used to capture pheasants.

○ Evaluate what type of father Danny had in the story.

○ Judge whether Danny and his father should be hunting pheasants.

○ Predict what life will be like as Danny becomes a teenager.

○ Why might Danny become an excellent hunter in the future?

○ What makes this story so enjoyable?

For The Love Of Gold

by Janelle Diller

Keziah is growing up in the wild, gold-rush boom town of Cripple Creek Colorado. Her family slowly succumbs to the lure of the good life that riches offer. The town is all but destroyed by fire, a strange miner threatens Keziah's life over gold, and the family mine costs more to work than it produces. But it is the slowly arrived at understanding of a neighboring family, newly awash in money but unable to help itself emotionally, that forces Keziah to see what is most important in life.

LEVEL 1 (KNOWLEDGE)

o Where does this story take place?

o What did Hairless Henry tell Keziah to tell her father?

o Who are the members of Keziah's family and what do they do?

o When does this story take place?

LEVEL 2 (COMPREHENSION)

o Summarize Gerda Schmieder's little rituals.

o Describe the destruction the fire wrought on Cripple Creek.

o Tell how gold mining was done in the 1890's.

o Summarize a typical family day for Keziah.

LEVEL 3 (APPLICATION)

o How do your responsibilities at home compare to Keziah's?

o If you were Keziah, how would you have handled the first encounter with Hairless Harry?

o Have you ever visited a mine? Describe.

o How would your parents react to a friend giving you expensive gifts that they themselves couldn't afford to give you?

LEVEL 4 (ANALYSIS)

o Analyze the type of person who would participate in a gold-rush and create a boom town. What would this community be like?

o Compare family size of the 1890's to today's family.

o Compare Keziah's family to the Schmieder family.

o What type of person was Erick?

o Analyze the relationship between Erick and Keziah.

o How would you describe Mose Picket? Cite examples to back up your opinion.

LEVEL 5 (SYNTHESIS)

o What would have happened to Keziah's family if their mine were a huge success?

o What would have happened to Keziah if Hairless Henry didn't go back to corroborate her story in Cripple Creek?

o What would happen to Mose Picket in court, if he survived?

o If this story were set in Alaska in the same time period, what would change?

o Suppose that grubstaking was declared illegal. What would be the affect on the number of mines?

o If Daniel chose to remain a carpenter, how would his family's fortunes be different?

LEVEL 6 (EVALUATION)

o Can money buy happiness?

o Evaluate Mary Margaret's attitude toward Miss Blade.

o In what way was Erick's gift of a coat to Keziah a slap in Daniel's face?

o What does friendship require?

o What is integrity?

o What makes Ethel Blade a survivor and a hero?

There's A Bat In Bunk Five

by Paula Danziger

When Marcy got the letter from Ms. Finney, she was thrilled. Ms. Finney was the best teacher Marcy had ever had—until the school fired her. And now she was asking Marcy to be a counselor-in-training at her creative arts camp. Marcy arrives at camp but doesn't bargain for being assigned to Bunk 5, the one with a bat, and Ginger, the problem camper!

LEVEL 1 (KNOWLEDGE)

○ Where was Marcy's new camp located?

○ Who gave Marcy lots of trouble in Bunk Five?

○ What boy did Marcy have a close friendship with?

○ What did Ginger do that upset everyone?

LEVEL 2 (COMPREHENSION)

○ Describe how Marcy felt about going to camp.

○ Describe Marcy's Bunk Five.

○ Explain what Ginger did that annoyed everyone.

○ Tell what Marcy liked most about camp.

LEVEL 3 (APPLICATION)

○ Have you ever gone to a sleep away camp? Explain.

○ How would you have handled the problem of Bunk Five?

○ What made you most angry about Marcy's camp situation?

o Would you have wanted to be in Bunk Five if you had gone to Marcy's camp? Why?

LEVEL 4 (ANALYSIS)

o Which event in the story caused Marcy the greatest frustration?

o What did Marcy like most about her camp experience?

o Compare Ginger with someone you know that always causes trouble.

o Analyze Marcy's responsibilities as a counselor in training.

o How would Marcy describe her camp experiences in a letter to her parents? Explain.

o Compare Marcy's camp to a camp you have gone to.

LEVEL 5 (SYNTHESIS)

o Will Marcy return to camp next year? Why?

o What else could have happened in Bunk Five?

o Think of a new name for Bunk Five.

o What types of punishment could someone like Ginger get at a real camp?

o If you were a counselor, what kind of rules would you have for your bunk?

o Describe how Marcy and Ginger will get along next year at camp.

LEVEL 6 (EVALUATION)

o Do Bunk Five situations really exist in camp?

o How do camp administrators handle someone like Ginger?

○ Judge whether Marcy will return to camp next year.

○ How could Bunk Five be made different?

○ How will Marcy describe her camp experience to her parents when she gets home?

○ Tell three reasons why Marcy will return to camp next year.

6th Grade Can Really Kill You

by Barthe DeClements

The friends of Elsie Edwards return for a year of disastrous fun in sixth grade. A new school year promises some terrifying hurdles for "Bad Helen," the self-confessed rowdiest kid in school. If Helen can't improve her reading skills, she'll be stuck in sixth grade forever, and her teacher, Mrs. Lobb, is no help at all.

LEVEL 1 (KNOWLEDGE)

○ Who was Helen's first sixth grade teacher?

○ What subject did Helen have great difficulty with?

○ What did Helen do outside the faculty room?

○ What did the school do to finally help Helen with her reading problem?

LEVEL 2 (COMPREHENSION)

○ Describe Helen's first encounter with Mrs. Lobb.

○ Describe the grades Helen received on her first report card.

○ Describe what Helen disliked about school.

○ Tell what other things Helen did to annoy her teachers.

LEVEL 3 (APPLICATION)

○ Would you like to be friends with Helen? Why?

○ Is Helen's school like your school? Explain.

○ Why did Helen think that sixth grade would kill her?

○ How would your parents react if you behaved like Helen?

LEVEL 4 (ANALYSIS)

○ Why did Helen fool around so much in school?

○ What was Mrs. Lobb's feelings toward Helen?

○ Which event in the story gave you a clear picture of what Helen was like?

○ Was Helen liked by her classmates?

○ Analyze the principal's actions toward Helen.

○ Compare Helen to someone you know who fools around in school.

LEVEL 5 (SYNTHESIS)

○ Design the perfect class for Helen.

○ Describe the perfect friend for Helen.

○ Suppose Helen was a gifted student. How would that have changed the story?

○ Name some things that Helen could do in the last month of school which could change everyone's impression of her.

○ Imagine that you were in Helen's sixth-grade class. What would you want to say to her?

○ You have just found Helen's secret diary. Tell what it says.

LEVEL 6 (EVALUATION)

○ Judge Mrs. Lobb as a teacher.

○ Did Helen's parents support her? If yes, how?

○ How is Helen's sixth grade like your sixth grade? Explain.

○ Decide whether you would want to be a close friend of Helen's.

○ Predict how Helen's reading problem will affect her performance in school.

○ Will Helen ever be able to go to college? Explain.

The Black Stallion

by Walter Farley

Alec Ramsay first saw the Black Stallion when his ship docked at a small Arabian port on the Red Sea. Little did he dream then that the magnificent wild horse was destined to play an important part in his young life; that the strange understanding which grew between them would lead them through untold dangers to high adventure in America.

LEVEL 1 (KNOWLEDGE)

○ Where did Alec first see the Black Stallion?

○ What happened to the Drake?

○ Who saved Alec's life?

○ Name the two horses the Black Stallion beat in Chicago.

LEVEL 2 (COMPREHENSION)

○ Explain how the Black Stallion saved Alec's life.

○ Describe how Alec and the Black Stallion survived on the small island.

○ Describe how Alec trained for the big race.

○ Tell how the Black Stallion won the race.

LEVEL 3 (APPLICATION)

○ Have you ever ridden a large horse? Describe the experience.

○ Could you have ridden the Black Stallion? Explain.

○ If the Black Stallion was yours, where would you keep him?

○ What kinds of things would you want to do with the Black Stallion if he were yours?

LEVEL 4 (ANALYSIS)

○ Explain why Alec was so lucky to be alive after the shipwreck.

○ Analyze Alec's personality. Describe what kind of boy he was in the story.

○ Compare the Black Stallion to a horse you are familiar with.

○ Analyze Alec's method of training for the big race.

○ Why did Napoleon have a calming effect on the Black Stallion? Explain.

○ Why did Alec want to race the Black Stallion? Explain.

LEVEL 5 (SYNTHESIS)

○ How long could Alec and the Black Stallion have survived on the small island? Why?

○ Think of some newspaper headlines describing Alec's adventure.

○ Name some places you would like to take the Black Stallion if he were yours.

○ Think of some other names for the Black Stallion.

○ What could have happened to Alec while stranded on the small island? Explain.

○ Tell about other adventures Alec and the Black Stallion will have in the future.

LEVEL 6 (EVALUATION)

o Judge whether the Black Stallion could have really saved Alec in the story.

o What if Alec was told that the Black Stallion had to stay on the island—how would he have reacted?

o How did Alec's parents handle the arrival of the Black Stallion?

o Predict whether the Black Stallion will run in other races in the future.

o How much money do you think the Black Stallion is worth?

o What impressed you the most about this adventure story? Explain.

Love, From The Fifth-Grade Celebrity

by Patricia Reilly Giff

For the first time since The Girl Who Knew It All, *Casey Valentine and Tracey Matson meet again. They'll be in fifth grade together! And Casey is sure she'll be elected class president. But to her surprise, it's Tracey who's elected. Casey and Tracey run head on into divided loyalties in this lighthearted and realistic story which shows that learning how to give and take is part of being best friends too.*

LEVEL 1 (KNOWLEDGE)

○ Where were Casey and Tracey spending the summer?

○ What did Tracey teach Casey to do?

○ What was Tracey elected for?

○ What problem did Tracey have?

LEVEL 2 (COMPREHENSION)

○ Describe how Tracey became so popular with her fifth-grade friends.

○ Describe Casey's reaction to Tracey's new popularity.

○ Tell how Casey embarrassed Tracey.

○ Explain how Casey and Tracey settled their differences.

LEVEL 3 (APPLICATION)

○ Have you ever experienced jealousy over another student's popularity or special talents? Explain.

○ If you were Casey, how could you have avoided the jealousy issue?

○ Do adults experience popularity problems? Explain.

○ Should Casey have acted as she did in the story? Explain.

LEVEL 4 (ANALYSIS)

○ Why did Casey have such a difficult time accepting Tracey's new popularity?

○ Which event in the story really demonstrated how Casey felt about Tracey's popularity?

○ Why did Tracey become so popular in her new school?

○ Compare Casey and Tracey's difficulties with two students you know who are experiencing similar problems.

○ Did you feel, early in the story, that the two girls would eventually make up? Why?

○ Why is this story so real?

LEVEL 5 (SYNTHESIS)

○ Suppose Casey was elected class president, how would that have changed the story?

○ Suppose there weren't any class elections. Would that have changed things? How?

○ Suppose Casey and Tracey were each fourteen years old. Would that have changed things? How?

○ Change the ending—create something different for how the girls solved their problem.

○ Tell how the story would be different if it had been two eleven-year-old boys.

○ Suppose the students realized Casey's jealousy. How might they have reacted toward her?

LEVEL 6 (EVALUATION)

○ Judge Casey's reasons for becoming angry with Tracey.

○ What makes this story a real life experience?

○ Decide whether Casey and Tracey will have difficulty getting along in the future.

○ What did you learn from this story? Explain.

○ Why should other students read this story?

○ Do you think class elections cause similar problems in other schools? How?

They Would Never Be Friends

by Lawrence and Suella Walsh

Basketball and making the school team was Amy's and Kim's dream since second grade. Finally they are in the eighth grade, and tryouts are scheduled. But Amy has broken her arm. Kim will have to make the dream come true for both of them and win her spot on the team beside the sophisticated, snooty and excellent player, Hillary, who she could never call "friend." For the good of the team, Kim has to learn to put her personal feelings about Hillary aside.

LEVEL 1 (KNOWLEDGE)

o How long have Kim and Amy been best friends?

o Why can't Amy try out?

o Who is Robin?

o What is Baxter?

LEVEL 2 (COMPREHENSION)

o Describe the girls in "the Group."

o Explain how Kim and Amy make a friend of Robin.

o Tell about Kim's assessment of Hillary's abilities.

o Describe some of Baxter's strong-arm maneuvers.

LEVEL 3 (APPLICATION)

o If you were on the team, with whom would you have a problem getting along?

o Who would you have chosen to start on the team?

o Have you ever played on a team with people who were not your friends? Did it affect your playing ability.

o How would you handle Baxter on the court?

LEVEL 4 (ANALYSIS)

o Analyze Robin's feelings towards her father.

o Compare Hillary's and Kim's playing style.

o What type of person was Amy?

o Analyze Hillary's attitude towards Kim.

o Which event in the story most reminded you of something you do with your friends?

o Why was the freshman class composed of such a diverse population of students?

LEVEL 5 (SYNTHESIS)

o How would the story be different if Amy had not broken her arm?

o Based on imaginary interviews with Hillary and Kim, create a feature story on teamwork for your school newspaper.

o What would have happened to the story if the refs were more on the ball about Baxter?

o Suppose something happened to coach in the middle of the season. What would happen to the team?

o Why are Kim, Robin and Amy a good team?

o Make up a scenario of the team's first game against Baxter next season with Amy on the team.

LEVEL 6 (EVALUATION)

o Judge how Baxter's bragging worked against them.

o Was the coach fair? Explain.

o What is friendship?

o Will Amy, Robin and Kim be more interested in boys than in basketball next year? Why do you think so?

o Who should be the team's player of the year?

o Which Baxter player bothered you the most?

The Death of Old Man Hanson

by David Kenneth Mull

The "neighborhood five" are determined to steal some apples from Old Man Hanson's orchard, but he foils every attempt they launch. Frustrated, they plan a series of pranks to distract him from the orchard. But the old man proves to be a master prankster himself, and the effects are shocking.

LEVEL 1 (KNOWLEDGE)

o Who are the "neighborhood five"?

o What are they after?

o What does G.O.H. stand for?

o Where does the story take place?

LEVEL 2 (COMPREHENSION)

o Describe Old Man Hanson's dog.

o Explain how one of the pranks the boys played on Old Man Hanson backfired.

o Describe what problem solving Sam and Bill had to do to get out of Old Man Hanson's house after they snooped their way in.

o Explain what happened to the boys when they turned eighteen years old.

LEVEL 3 (APPLICATION)

o Would you like to join the boys in their duel of wits with Old Man Hanson?

o Have you ever seen a hologram? Describe it.

o If you lived next door to Old Man Hanson, what would you think of him as a neighbor?

o Which of Old Man Hanson's pranks did you find most interesting?

LEVEL 4 (ANALYSIS)

o Analyze the type of pranks Old Man Hanson played. What would you say about his sense of fun?

o Compare Hanson's mental agility with that of someone you know who is his age.

o Why do the boys keep trying to steal Hanson's apples?

o Analyze the boys' pranks. Were they mean-spirited? What could you say about the boys?

o Do you think that Hanson liked smart kids? Explain.

o Why was Old Man Hanson living alone?

LEVEL 5 (SYNTHESIS)

o How would the story change if Old Man Hanson was nasty?

o Would the story be different if Old Man Hanson had a wife and children? Explain.

o How would you feel on the day before you turned eighteen and had to choose your replacement?

o The first Hanson benefactors were boys. How would you feel about being the first boy to choose a little girl to take your place?

o Do girls play pranks on their friends, or is it a macho thing?

o How could Old Man Hanson have rid himself of the boys at any time, if he really wanted to?

LEVEL 6 (EVALUATION)

o Were the boys or Old Man Hanson better at pranking?

o How do we know that Old Man Hanson actually enjoyed the boys antics?

o What was the motivating force behind Old Man Hanson's gift?

o How did Hanson's age give him an edge on the boys?

o Judge Old Man Hanson's stipulation for college tuition, then decide what his academic interests probably were. Explain.

o How do you suppose Hanson made his money?

Old Ladies With Brooms Aren't Always Witches

by Paula Woolf

Sixth grader Sarah Jane has just moved to town. Her new friends tell her to stay away from the house with the green door and the odd old woman who lives there. But Sarah Jane's curiosity pushes her up to and through the green door and into a surprising relationship with the strange woman.

LEVEL 1 (KNOWLEDGE)

o Describe Speck.

o Why does Sarah Jane use two names?

o How long has Sarah Jane lived in the Texas suburb?

o Who lives in the house with the green door?

LEVEL 2 (COMPREHENSION)

o What happened on Halloween to move Sarah Jane to action?

o In what ways was the woman a recluse?

o Describe how the puppy will help the woman to come out of her shell.

o Tell how Sarah Jane planned to foster a friendship with the old woman.

LEVEL 3 (APPLICATION)

o Have you had the experience of moving to a new town and a new school? What did you feel?

o Have you known anyone to be as helpful as Speck to a new friend?

o Have you ever seen a friend blinded by jealousy? Explain.

o Do sixth grade boys often befriend sixth grade girls?

LEVEL 4 (ANALYSIS)

o Why is Sarah Jane more interested than any of the other youngsters in the house with the green door?

o How is Sarah Jane like any new girl in town?

o Why did Sarah Jane persevere in her friendship with the old woman?

o Why did the old woman shut herself away in the first place?

o What must the old woman have gone through emotionally to come to hear Sarah Jane's speech?

LEVEL 5 (SYNTHESIS)

o If Speck had not warned Sarah Jane about the old woman, would Sarah Jane have been so interested in her?

o If Sarah Jane had been busy with her own social life, would she still have begun her friendship with the old woman?

o What would have happened if the girl's jacket had not been returned?

o If crayons were toxic, what would have happened to the five-year-old boy at the baby-sitting coop?

o Would the story change if Sarah Jane gave the woman a kitten rather than a puppy?

o What would have happened if the baby-sitting venture had failed to make a profit?

LEVEL 6 (EVALUATION)

o Predict if Sarah Jane's jealous classmate will turn out to be her best friend.

o How did Speck know how to relate to the five-year-old boy?

o Are cooperative baby sitting ventures usually a guaranteed success? Explain.

o Which one wants their friendship more, Sarah Jane or the old woman?

o Are Halloween pranks OK?

o Predict if Sarah Jane and Speck will date. Explain.

A Girl Called Al

by Constance C. Greene

*There's a new girl who moved down the hall from us. She said,
"Call me Al." Al is a little on the fat side, a non-conformist,
but a very interesting person. And this is the beginning of a warm,
funny, utterly real story of the friendship between two girls in a
city apartment house.*

LEVEL 1 (KNOWLEDGE)

○ With whom did Al live?

○ Whom did the two girl's like to visit?

○ Where did Al's father like to send her?

○ What was Al's real name?

LEVEL 2 (COMPREHENSION)

○ Describe what Al looked like.

○ Tell what the girls enjoyed doing when they were not in school.

○ Explain what Mr. Richardson would give the girls to eat when
they visited him.

○ Describe what happened to Mr. Richardson at the end of the
story.

LEVEL 3 (APPLICATION)

○ Do you know anyone who lives in a city apartment house?
Tell about them.

○ Tell why you would like Al for a friend.

○ What things did the girls do that you would enjoy doing?

○ Do you have a friend like Mr. Richardson? Explain.

LEVEL 4 (ANALYSIS)

○ Describe the event in the story which demonstrated the relationship the girls had.

○ Compare the two girls in terms of personality.

○ How was Al's mother different from the other girl's mother? Explain.

○ Why was Mr. Keogh such a nice teacher?

○ Which event in the story made you wish you were there?

○ Compare living in the city to living in the country.

LEVEL 5 (SYNTHESIS)

○ Name some activities you know the girls would enjoy doing.

○ Why did Al's mother and father get divorced? Explain.

○ Describe some funny nicknames that friends of yours have.

○ Name some things the girls could have done for their friend Mr. Richardson.

○ Tell about what you and the two girls would like to do in the city.

○ What do you think Al's friend's name was?

LEVEL 6 (EVALUATION)

○ Why was the relationship between the two girls a good one?

○ What things did the girls do that demonstrated kindness?

o Judge whether you would have wanted to live in the apartment house described in the story.

o Judge why Al was not a real good student.

o Predict what kind of friendship the girls will have in the future.

o Will there be another Mr. Richardson in their lives in the future?

Death Be Not Proud: A Memoir

by John Gunther

Johnny Gunther was seventeen years old when he died of a brain tumor. During the months of his final illness, everyone near him was unforgettably impressed by his level-headed courage, his wit and quiet friendliness, and, above all, by his unfaltering patience. This deeply moving book is a father's memoir of a brave, intelligent, and spirited boy.

LEVEL 1 (KNOWLEDGE)

○ Where was Johnny born?

○ Name the different places where Johnny lived his life.

○ What musical instrument did Johnny learn to master?

○ What caused Johnny's death?

LEVEL 2 (COMPREHENSION)

○ Describe Johnny's hobbies.

○ Describe Johnny's personality as told by his teachers.

○ Explain the personal things which caused Johnny problems.

○ Tell how Johnny was able to handle his illness.

LEVEL 3 (APPLICATION)

○ Have you ever known a young person with a serious illness? Explain.

○ How would you have accepted Johnny as a friend and classmate?

o Which of Johnny's characteristics did you most admire?

o What did you learn from this account of the life and death of Johnny Gunther?

LEVEL 4 (ANALYSIS)

o What did Johnny seem to enjoy most about life?

o Compare Johnny with someone you know who has great courage.

o Compare Johnny to someone you know who is very gifted.

o What was the most difficult thing about Johnny's illness?

o Which event in the story really gave you the impression of the quality of person Johnny was?

o Analyze Johnny's father's motives for writing this book.

LEVEL 5 (SYNTHESIS)

o What would Johnny have liked about your school program? Explain.

o Tell what you would have shared about yourself had you been friends with Johnny.

o Which teacher in your school would have found Johnny to be absolutely fascinating?

o Had Johnny lived a long life, what types of contributions could he have possibly made?

o Describe what would really interest Johnny if he lived in today's world.

o Describe what Johnny would have wanted written on his tombstone.

LEVEL 6 (EVALUATION)

○ Judge whether Johnny's parents were supportive of a gifted child.

○ Had Johnny lived to be an adult, which aspect of life would he have made the most contributions in—technology, arts, or humanism? Why?

○ What areas of education would Johnny most enjoy about our current school system?

○ Why is this an important book for young people to read?

○ What do you think was the main motivating force behind the writing of this book by Johnny's father?

○ Do you think that this book will remain a classic forever? Why?

The Outsiders

by S. E. Hinton

The story is about a fourteen-year-old boy, his two brothers—Darrel, twenty and Soda, sixteen—and their constant struggle to protect their territorial rights in an inner-city environment. Their hardships, fights, even tragedies are explicitly told in this true-to-life gang war type story. The ugly realities are descriptively presented in this drama.

LEVEL 1 (KNOWLEDGE)

○ What were the boy's brothers names?

○ Where did they live?

○ What happened to their parents?

○ What tragedy had a great impact on the boy?

LEVEL 2 (COMPREHENSION)

○ Describe what life was like living in the inner city.

○ Describe the events that took place which left a boy dead on the streets.

○ Explain how the boy and Johnny saved the lives of some young children.

○ Tell what happened to young Johnny.

LEVEL 3 (APPLICATION)

○ Have you heard stories about gang wars? Explain.

○ Have you traveled through neighborhoods where gangs of teen-agers live? Explain.

- If you had been the boy in the story, how would you have protected yourself from danger?

- How does your community prevent teenagers from fighting in gangs? Explain.

LEVEL 4 (ANALYSIS)

- Compare the boy's two brothers.

- Why would the boy want to be in the streets at night all alone?

- Which event in the story made you realize the seriousness of the boy's situation?

- Compare the boy's life with your lifestyle.

- Analyze the boy's decision to run away with Johnny.

- Why were the gangs always battling? Explain.

LEVEL 5 (SYNTHESIS)

- Having both parents alive, how might the boy's experiences be different?

- Suppose the boy carried a weapon. What might have happened?

- Suppose the boy had been clean looking. Would he have gotten into so much trouble?

- Where else could the boy and Johnny have run?

- How could the brothers have been more protective of their younger brother? Explain.

- If you could have met the boy, what kinds of things would you want to have said to him?

LEVEL 6 (EVALUATION)

○ Judge the supervision the older brothers gave their younger brother.

○ Why is this story a true-to-life account of certain neighborhoods?

○ Evaluate whether the police did all they could do to protect the neighborhood.

○ Why might the boy be taken from the custody of his older brothers?

○ What thoughts do you have about life in a neighborhood like the one in the story? Explain.

○ Decide what the boy's life will be like in the future.

The Secret of Poplar Island

by Beth Deemer

Josh and Teague, both twelve, explore a mysterious island. When their boat sinks, they are at the mercy of the island's only inhabitant. Their friendship with him turns out to be much more a life-changing force than they'd ever imagined.

LEVEL 1 (KNOWLEDGE)

o What is the name of the island?

o What are some of the stories told about the island?

o What is the name of Melvin's boat?

o What does Melvin farm?

LEVEL 2 (COMPREHENSION)

o Why does Melvin live on the island?

o Explain how the boys plan to raise the money they need to buy and fix up a boat.

o Describe the business Melvin and the boys create.

o Explain how Josh got suckered in by Jimmy when he purchased the scow.

LEVEL 3 (APPLICATION)

o Have you ever wondered who lives on little off-shore islands?

o How do oyster and rockfish beds help the environment?

o Why should a purchaser always get title papers from the seller when buying a used car or boat?

o Why is it dangerous to live alone on an island?

LEVEL 4 (ANALYSIS)

o Why did the boys go to the island in the first place?

o Why did Josh go ahead with his purchase of a boat from Jimmy even though he knew Jimmy's history of dishonesty?

o Why did Melvin want to go into business with the boys?

o Why was the president's boat housed in Poplar Island?

o What made the oyster and rockfish business such a success?

LEVEL 5 (SYNTHESIS)

o What would have happened to Melvin had he not met Josh and Teague?

o What would be different about the island if no one lived on it?

o Do you know anyone with Josh's ability around small engines?

o How would the story change if it were set in a cove instead of an island?

o Would the story work if Josh were Jane?

o What would have happened if Josh couldn't get the Goose to run?

LEVEL 6 (EVALUATION)

o Judge Melvin's character.

o What did the boys learn from their business experience?

o How did the island's secret remain undiscovered for so long?

o Why was Melvin such a good listener?

o In what ways was the business an equal partnership?

o Which character profited most from the relationship? Josh? Teague? Melvin?

Dark Things

by Joseph Brown

A boy of magic and a boy versed in computer technology meet and share their interests in creating horror games. Tony's horrors can be turned off, but Jarrod's monster escapes, and Jarrod must use all of his powers to recapture it.

LEVEL 1 (KNOWLEDGE)

o As a partner in his father's act, what does Jarrod do?

o How does Jarrod escape his father's fate?

o When did Tony and Jarrod meet?

o How old is Jarrod in 1997?

LEVEL 2 (COMPREHENSION)

o Describe The Root.

o How does the Ophelia horror box work?

o Tell how Jarrod stays youthful.

o Describe Jarrod's transport Craft.

LEVEL 3 (APPLICATION)

o How does having the same interests add to a friendship?

o Have you ever imagined your own, private monster?

o Would Jarrod's Root be able to exist where you live?

o Where would you go if you could ride in Jarrod's Craft?

LEVEL 4 (ANALYSIS)

o How is Tony like an average kid?

o Why is it that Tony and Jarrod get along so well?

o Analyze what was wrong with Jarrod's money.

o Why aren't Tony's parents afraid of Jarrod?

o Why is the balloon ride in The Root dangerous?

o In what ways is Jarrod like an average kid?

LEVEL 5 (SYNTHESIS)

o What other names cold Jarrod have given his home?

o Which of your computer games would the boys enjoy playing?

o Could Tony be popular in your class?

o Why can only Jarrod get rid of the dark thing?

o Would you want to go on a vacation with Jarrod?

LEVEL 6 (EVALUATION)

o Why would Jarrod fit in with the Magellan family?

o Is the Ophelia Box a good investment for an amusement park?

o Judge whether Jarrod will allow himself to age as Tony does.

o Can Jarrod find happiness as a normal boy?

o Judge if The Root takes care of Jarrod as a parent would. Is this friendship?

Make Me Disappear

by Cameron Kent

Ten-year-old apprentice magician Sam persuades a real magician to get him into Wundriana, the place where everything that is lost or banished goes. Sam is planning to run away because his father is going to marry the phony Cynthia, who wants Sam far away in boarding school. But in Wundriana Sam finds knowledge, the beautiful Kristina, the evil Sinjin, and the need to go home again to the real world.

LEVEL 1 (KNOWLEDGE)

o What does Sam's birthday mean to magicians?

o What does Cynthia want Sam's father to do with Sam?

o Who is Choko the Clown really?

o How did Sinjin get to Wundriana?

LEVEL 2 (COMPREHENSION)

o Describe Sam's feelings about magic.

o Describe how Cynthia has been making Sam's life miserable.

o Tell how Sam outwits Sinjin.

o Explain how Sam's disappearance shakes up his father.

LEVEL 3 (APPLICATION)

o How would you handle a phony like Cynthia fooling your parents?

o Have you ever wanted to run away? Explain.

o Would you accept Sam as a friend?

o If you had an apprentice magician, would you teach him how to get to Wundriana?

LEVEL 4 (ANALYSIS)

o What type of person was The Great Blackwell LaVeque?

o What did the plastic Christmas tree mean to Sam's father?

o Why could Blackwell's magic book be dangerous?

o Analyze Kristina's feelings when she sees that Blackwell is too weak to bring Sam home with his magic.

o Which event in the story shows that Sam is really clever?

o What are Sam's feelings towards Kristina?

LEVEL 5 (SYNTHESIS)

o Will Sam ever return to Wundriana? Why?

o What would have become of Sam if he stayed in Wundriana?

o What will become of Kristina in the real world?

o If Sam's father never met Cynthia, how would the story change?

o Describe what it was like in Wundriana for Kristina.

o If Sam's birthday was not October 31, how would the story change?

LEVEL 6 (EVALUATION)

o Judge Sam's father's qualities.

o What is the setting of most magic stories?

o Why are magicians interesting people?

o Should Blackwell have shown Sam how to get to Wundriana?

o Evaluate Wundriana as a good or a bad place.

o What does this story tell you about running away?

From The Mixed-Up Files Of Mrs. Basil E. Frankweiler

by E. L. Konigsburg

When Claudia decided to run away, she planned very carefully. She would be gone just long enough to teach her parents a lesson in Claudia appreciation. And she would go in comfort—she would live at the Metropolitan Museum of Art. While at the museum, Claudia and her brother, Jamie, become intrigued by Michelangelo's statue, Angel. The quest for more information leads them to the former owner of the statue, Mrs. Basil E. Frankweiler. Without her—well, without her, Claudia might never have found a way to go home.

LEVEL 1 (KNOWLEDGE)

○ Where did Claudia and Jamie sleep while at the museum?

○ What was the name of the statue created by Michelangelo?

○ Where did Claudia and Jamie eat their meals during their stay at the museum?

○ How did the children get to Mrs. Frankweiler's house?

○ What piece of evidence did Claudia find about the statue, Angel?

LEVEL 2 (COMPREHENSION)

○ Explain how Claudia and Jamie got to the museum.

○ Describe what they did during the day time.

○ Explain why they sent the museum a letter.

○ Tell what they found at Mrs. Frankweiler's house.

LEVEL 3 (APPLICATION)

○ Have you ever thought about running away? Explain.

○ If you spent a few days hiding in the Metropolitan Museum of Art, what would you do with your time?

○ What is something in life that you have a tremendous curiosity about?

○ How will Claudia's parents handle the event?

LEVEL 4 (ANALYSIS)

○ Analyze Claudia's parents' feelings the night she and Jamie disappeared.

○ Compare this run away situation to a run away situation you have heard about in your community.

○ Which event in the story would have been the most difficult for you to handle?

○ Relate this story to any thoughts you might have had about running away.

○ Describe the relationship between Mrs. Frankweiler and her attorney, Mr. Saxonberg.

○ Analyze the relationship between Claudia and Jamie.

LEVEL 5 (SYNTHESIS)

○ Suppose Claudia and Jamie were caught by the museum guards. What would have happened?

○ What could have happened to Claudia and Jamie while walking around New York City?

○ Think of a new story title.

○ Think of a situation that really could have scared the children while at the museum.

○ Create several newspaper headlines about the missing children.

○ Create several newspaper headlines after the children returned home.

LEVEL 6 (EVALUATION)

○ Judge Claudia's decision to run away.

○ Judge Claudia's decision to take her nine year old brother with her.

○ If a twelve year old and a nine year old had hid in the museum, would children of that age, study, explore, and research the exhibits? Why?

○ What punishment will the children receive from their parents?

○ What does this story tell you about the curiosity of a young mind?

○ Predict whether Claudia and Jamie will visit Mrs. Frankweiler again.

Jennifer, Hecate, MacBeth, William McKinley, And Me, Elizabeth

by E. L. Lonigsburg

Elizabeth is the loneliest only child in the whole U.S. of A. until she discovers Jennifer. Of course, Jennifer isn't a friend, really. Witches don't make friends, and Jennifer is a witch. Elizabeth becomes her apprentice, however, and in the process of learning how to become a witch herself, she also learns how to eat raw eggs, how to cast short spells, and how to get along with Jennifer, among other things.

LEVEL 1 (KNOWLEDGE)

○ What was Jennifer practicing?

○ Where did Elizabeth find notes from Jennifer?

○ What book did Jennifer suggest that Elizabeth read?

○ Where did Jennifer and Elizabeth spend Saturdays?

LEVEL 2 (COMPREHENSION)

○ Describe what Elizabeth had to eat as an apprentice witch.

○ Describe Jennifer's personality and behavior.

○ Tell what some of the taboos were which Elizabeth had to follow in becoming a master witch.

○ Tell what happened when the girls began to make their magical ointment.

LEVEL 3 (APPLICATION)

○ Would you like to study witchcraft with Jennifer?

- If you were Elizabeth and your parents found out about being a witch's apprentice, how would they have reacted to the situation?

- Have you ever heard of kids practicing witchcraft? Explain.

- Why might it be dangerous to practice something like witchcraft?

LEVEL 4 (ANALYSIS)

- Where do you think Jennifer learned witchcraft?

- Which event in the story demonstrated the negative aspect of something like witchcraft?

- Why would your friends avoid getting involved in witchcraft?

- Why would Jennifer be a hard person to make friends with?

- Which event in the story demonstrated the true Elizabeth?

- Do you think Jennifer would have wanted additional children to become witches had she continued her practice? Why?

LEVEL 5 (SYNTHESIS)

- Think of other taboos Jennifer could have given Elizabeth.

- Suppose the principal found out what the girls were doing. What might have happened?

- Why are there probably other children practicing some form of witchcraft?

- How would your mom be as an apprentice witch? Explain.

- Which relative in your family would find witchcraft interesting? Why?

- Think of a new ending to the story.

LEVEL 6 (EVALUATION)

○ Tell why witchcraft is dangerous.

○ Which aspect of witchcraft did you find unpleasant?

○ Which aspect of witchcraft was most interesting?

○ Judge why Jennifer decided to give up witchcraft.

○ Predict whether Jennifer will ever return to practicing witch-craft.

○ Predict what Jennifer and Elizabeth's relationship will be like in the future.

Ben And Me

by Robert Lawson

This is the book in which Amos (a mouse) immodestly reveals that he, Dr. Franklin's closest friend and advisor, was largely responsible for the great man's inventions, discoveries, and successes, especially at the French Court.

LEVEL 1 (KNOWLEDGE)

○ Who is Amos?

○ Where did Amos live?

○ What was Ben Franklin's first invention in the story?

○ How did Ben Franklin discover electricity?

○ Which foreign country did Dr. Franklin help?

LEVEL 2 (COMPREHENSION)

○ Describe where Ben Franklin lived.

○ Describe how the first Franklin stove was made.

○ Explain how Amos assisted Ben Franklin in discovering electricity.

○ Tell how Ben Franklin helped the French government.

LEVEL 3 (APPLICATION)

○ Have you ever visited the Franklin Museum in Philadelphia? Describe it.

○ Which event in the story did you find most interesting? Why?

- If you had lived next to Ben Franklin, what would you have thought of him as your neighbor?

- Why did you find Ben Franklin such an interesting person? Explain.

LEVEL 4 (ANALYSIS)

- What type of an individual was Ben Franklin?

- Which invention made Ben Franklin the most famous?

- How did Ben Franklin protect his inventions?

- Why was Ben Franklin such a successful good-will ambassador to France?

- Compare Ben Franklin to George Washington.

- Compare life in Philadelphia in the late 1700's to Philadelphia today.

LEVEL 5 (SYNTHESIS)

- Why did Amos feel he was responsible for Ben Franklin's inventions?

- In what areas did Ben Franklin not invent anything?

- What predictions would Ben Franklin have made about the future?

- What would be Ben Franklin's reaction to today's technology?

- Can you name any modern day Ben Franklin's?

- Why would you like to have been Ben Franklin's child?

LEVEL 6 (EVALUATION)

- Judge what kind of person Ben Franklin was.

- Evaluate the manner in which Ben Franklin lived in Philadelphia.

- Judge how Ben Franklin got his ideas.

- What made Ben Franklin so famous? Explain.

- Predict what he would have accomplished had he lived for another fifty years.

- Why will the memories of Ben Franklin live forever?

A Wrinkle In Time

by Madeleine L'Engle

A Wrinkle In Time is all about an imaginative journey that three young children experience. This unique and unusual story allows one's fantasy to take off! It is a fantastic voyage of the world beyond!

LEVEL 1 (KNOWLEDGE)

○ What three children search for the tesseract?

○ Who are the three ladies (witches in the story)?

○ Where do the children find their father?

○ What is a tesseract?

LEVEL 2 (COMPREHENSION)

○ Describe how the children are taken from their home.

○ Describe their amazing journey through space and time.

○ Tell how they found their father.

○ Explain the special powers the witches used in the story.

LEVEL 3 (APPLICATION)

○ How is this story like a bad dream you've had?

○ Describe your most vivid images as you read the story.

○ What thing or aspect of the story would you like to write about? Why?

○ Who would like this story more—your mother or father? Why?

LEVEL 4 (ANALYSIS)

○ Why was it necessary to have three witches in the story?

○ Which child had the most difficulty with this wrinkle in time? Why?

○ Which of the three witches did you least like? Why?

○ Compare this story to another imaginative journey you have read.

○ Define what a tesseract is and tell what you learned from this experience.

○ Analyze the main point of the story.

LEVEL 5 (SYNTHESIS)

○ Tell about a fourth witch in the story. Describe her including her powers.

○ Describe the type of music you would use as background if you were reading this book to an audience.

○ Create a new title for this story. Be original.

○ Suppose Mrs. Murry went with the children in the wrinkle of time. How might that have changed the story?

○ Having read this story, what might you dream about in the near future? Explain.

○ Who in your class would have loved to have been on this trip? Why?

LEVEL 6 (EVALUATION)

○ Why is the author of *A Wrinkle In Time* a very creative person? Explain.

94

o Judge whether you would have acted like the children in the story had you been on the trip.

o What might you change about this story? Explain.

o Name some things that you were familiar with in the story, especially during the wrinkle in time part.

o Describe whether you would recommend that all fifth and sixth graders read this story. Why?

o The most important thing I learned from this story was....

The Lion, The Witch, And The Wardrobe

by C. S. Lewis

Welcome to Narnia, a delightfully magical land where talking animals, fawns, dwarfs, and friendly giants live in peace and harmony. When four English school children find their way into this mysterious other world, they are struck by a scene of dazzling snow—cold, silent, and forbidding. The children's strange and unexpected adventures are climaxed in a glorious and fierce battle in which they aid the lion king in his triumph over the White Witch.

LEVEL 1 (KNOWLEDGE)

○ Name the four children in the fairy tale.

○ What was the name of the magical land they visited?

○ Who became the children's friend during their adventure?

○ Who triumphed over the White Witch?

LEVEL 2 (COMPREHENSION)

○ Describe life in Narnia as the children saw it.

○ Describe the actions of the White Witch. How did she cause the children problems?

○ Tell how Aslan, the golden lion, defeats the White Witch.

○ Describe what the children enjoyed most about their adventure.

LEVEL 3 (APPLICATION)

○ What does this fairy tale make you think of in children's literature?

○ What character in the story would you most like to be? Why?

○ Which event in the story would you most like to draw? Why?

○ What color comes to your mind when you think about this story? Why?

LEVEL 4 (ANALYSIS)

○ Compare Narnia to a place you are familiar with.

○ Where did the Wardrobe get its magic from?

○ Why was the White Witch such a mean character?

○ What did the children have difficulty understanding about their adventure in Narnia? Explain.

○ Compare this story with another fairy tale you have read.

○ Compare the White Witch to the witch in Snow White.

LEVEL 5 (SYNTHESIS)

○ Think of ways you could have gotten rid of the White Witch.

○ What did the children learn from all the animals of Narnia?

○ What made Aslan such a wise and gracious ruler? Explain.

○ Name three people you would like to take to Narnia.

○ Rename Narnia. Think of a new name for this kingdom.

○ Think of some things the children could have brought with them to make the journey into Narnia more fun.

LEVEL 6 (EVALUATION)

○ Judge why Aslan was made ruler of Narnia.

○ What three events would you eliminate from the story? Why?

- How would you rate the children's reactions and behavior during their visit to Narnia?

- Which part of the story was the most imaginative? Why?

- Evaluate the authors sequence of events while the children explored Narnia.

- Why is this a good book for stimulating the imagination? Explain.

Stray Cat

by Linda Rae Apolozon

Katrina's fifth grade teacher doesn't appreciate her atypical questions and boredom in class that leads her to misbehaving. Her parents send her to a private school for bright youngsters, where she discovers that her creativity and intellect are welcomed. Now, her problem is to learn how to make friends.

LEVEL 1 (KNOWLEDGE)

o In what grade is Katrina?

o Why was her mother frequently summoned to school?

o What does Katrina think of the Margaret James School at first?

o What is Amy Nishi's hidden talent?

LEVEL 2 (COMPREHENSION)

o Describe Katrina's attitude towards change.

o Explain how Katrina first begins to fit in at the Margaret James School.

o Describe Decimal's brush with death.

o Describe Amy Nishi's home.

LEVEL 3 (APPLICATION)

o Have you ever been an outsider to a group you wanted to join? Explain.

o What was Amy's problem at Katrina's sleepover?

o Would you want Katrina as a friend?

o Would you want to wear a school uniform?

LEVEL 4 (ANALYSIS)

o Compare Katrina's teacher in public school to Katrina's teacher in the Margaret James School.

o Compare Katrina to a smart fifth grader you know.

o Why was the public school teacher uncomfortable with Katrina in her class?

o Why did Amy hide her talents as a composer?

o Compare Katrina's mother to your mother in responding to her child's school problems.

o What could Katrina have done to stay out of trouble in public school?

LEVEL 5 (SYNTHESIZES)

o Is there an alternative to public school and private school? Do you know anyone being home-schooled?

o If this story were set in the 1890's what would happen to Katrina's education?

o Redesign Katrina's school uniform.

o If Decimal could talk, what might he say to Katrina?

o What would you suggest Katrina do in high school?

o Besides Amy, who do you think Katrina will become friendly with? Explain.

LEVEL 6 (EVALUATION)

o Judge Katrina's character.

o Do you think Amy and Katrina will become long-term good friends?

o How can public schools adjust their curriculum to keep bright students interested?

o Predict what kind of life Decimal can expect as Katrina's pet.

o Is it normal for preteen girls to be shy?

o If you were a guidance counselor and Katrina came to you with a problem about making friends, what would you tell her?

Taking Control

by Ann Love

During a class trip to a museum, Julian is bored and wanders away from the group and meets Mr. Callisthenes who offers to teach him about Alexander The Great by taking him back in time to various points in Alexander's life. Julian becomes a part of history. He confides in his sister, and luckily Mr. Callisthenes agrees to include Melanie in their trips. There is more to history than meets the reader's or museum visitor's eye.

LEVEL 1 (KNOWLEDGE)

o Where did Julia meet Mr. Callisthenes?

o What was the deal that Mr. Callisthenes offered Julian?

o Who was Achilles?

o What happened to King Philip, Alexander's father?

LEVEL 2 (COMPREHENSION)

o Explain why Julian confides in his sister, Melanie.

o Describe Julian's reaction to the taking of Tyre, and the slaughter.

o Tell why Alexander decided to return to Macedonia.

o Explain how living in Alexander's time helped Julian understand and appreciate museums and their role in preserving history.

LEVEL 3 (APPLICATION)

o Would you have gone with Mr. Callisthenes the first time?

o Would you have time traveled with him again after learning more about his character?

o How would you have retrieved the ring?

o Which episode in the story would you like to visit most? Why?

o What is the most memorable thing that you learned about Alexander The Great?

LEVEL 4 (ANALYSIS)

o Compare Alexander with another warrior hero you have studied.

o What caused Alexander's death?

o What was the relationship between Mr. Calisthenes and Alexander?

o Compare Melanie to you own brother or sister.

o What was the significance of Alexander's victory over Darius at the Battle of Issus?

o Analyze Alexander's feelings about the Oracle of Ammon in Siwa.

LEVEL 5 (SYNTHESIS)

o Can you name any modern day Alexanders? Who?

o Suppose Julian did not get his ring back. What would happen?

o How would the story change if Melanie was not with her brother?

o How would you describe Alexander if you were Darius?

o Why did Mr. Callisthenes feel responsible to make Alexander's story known?

o How can Julian and Melanie learn more about Alexander and his world without Mr. Callisthenes?

LEVEL 6 (EVALUATION)

o Which episode was the most dangerous for Julian?

o Judge Callisthenes' actions and motivations in Alexander's time.

o Is slaughtering the enemy necessary to win a war?

o Predict if Mr. Callisthenes will appear in the museum again for another bored student.

o How do you know Julian and Melanie enjoyed a good relationship?

o Was Julian and Melanie's father aware and responsible?

Trapped!

by Eunice Boeve

The true story of Virginia Reed, who, with her family and the Donners, faced incredible hardships on an overland journey from Illinois to California in 1846. The story chronicles the events as they happened. Only the dialog has been invented in this true adventure story of survival.

LEVEL 1 (KNOWLEDGE)

o Look at a map of the United States and draw with your finger a line from Springfield, Illinois, over the Sierra Mountains on to California.

o Who discovered a new, shorter route than the well known one?

o How many wagons turned off onto the new route?

o When did they begin climbing the high Sierra Mountains?

LEVEL 2 (COMPREHENSION)

o Describe how the wagon trains got through the forests.

o Tell what happened as the party crossed the desert.

o Describe the problems in the deep snow of the Sierras.

o Explain how the family tried to ward off starvation in the mountains.

LEVEL 3 (APPLICATION)

o How would you have felt about leaving your loved pet behind?

o Do you think you could have survived as Virginia did? Explain.

o Describe your most vivid images as you read the story.

o Tell about an experience you've had being very cold or very hungry, or both.

LEVEL 4 (ANALYSIS)

o Analyze the relationship between Virginia and her father.

o Why did the group consider Virginia's father guilty of murder?

o Compare your local winter to a Sierra Mountains winter.

o Why shouldn't a person who has been starving eat a big meal as soon as possible?

o How would you describe Virginia's personality?

o Why did the group throw Virginia's father out to fend for himself?

LEVEL 5 (SYNTHESIS)

o How would the story be different if the party stayed on the original trail?

o What would have happened to Billy if he had not been left behind?

o If mother had continued to languish, what would have become of the family?

o Would you have voted to shift to the new route? Explain.

o If Virginia were alive today, would she be popular in school? Explain.

LEVEL 6 (EVALUATION)

o Why is this an important book for young people to read?

o Judge Virginia's mother on her actions to save the family.

o This is a true story, only the dialog has been added. Is the dialog a success?

o Did Hastings try to help the wagons sufficiently?

o Is it worse to die from cold, or from starvation?

The Call Of The Wild

by Jack London

A remarkable dog, named Buck, tells of his life and near death experiences with man and beast in the great Yukon. A magnificent adventure, capturing the essence of survival and the relationship between man and dog. A true adventure written in a masterful way.

LEVEL 1 (KNOWLEDGE)

O Who was Buck's original owner?

O Where was Buck first taken to?

O What dog did Buck have to kill to become leader of the pack?

O Who did Buck really love in the story?

LEVEL 2 (COMPREHENSION)

O Describe how Buck's captives taught him how to obey.

O Tell how Buck became leader of the pack.

O Describe one of Buck's trips through the Yukon.

O Explain how Buck lost his master.

LEVEL 3 (APPLICATION)

O Have you ever known a dog like Buck?

O How would you have tried to find Buck if he had been stolen from you?

O Why is a dog considered to be man's best friend?

O How does this story eafect your feelings toward dogs?

LEVER 4 (ANALYSIS)

○ How else could Buck have been trained instead of clubbing him?

○ Which event really demonstrated the savagery of the Northland?

○ Analyze why Buck was such a great leader.

○ How did Buck show a good level of intelligence for a dog?

○ Why was it difficult to properly feed the team of dogs during the long trips through the Yukon?

○ What were Buck's greatest personal strengths?

LEVEL 5 (SYNTHESIS)

○ Suppose Buck wasn't as trusting, might his kidnapping never occurred? Explain.

○ Tell how a dog survives in the mighty Northland.

○ How would you have gotten food for your team of dogs?

○ Describe what kind of food Buck needed to remain strong and healthy in the Northland.

○ Think of some other titles for this great adventure story.

○ Suppose you had been John Thornton's child. How would you have looked after Buck?

LEVEL 6 (EVALUATION)

○ Why would pulling a sled be difficult for a dog in the great Northland?

○ Why weren't the police more involved in preventing the sales of stolen dogs?

o Could a dog have really survived all that Buck did? Why?

o Judge why Buck found Mr. Thornton to be a great master.

o What makes this story a real classic?

o What three things did you learn from this adventure?

Way of the Topi

by Thomas Anderson

Brother and sister Tim and Lisa are conservation activists. They are visiting their friends Kabedi and Tumba and their family, who live in a small African village on the savannah. When Tim insists that there seems to be a lack of large, wild animals, the group of four gets involved in a dangerous search that leads them into a bone-filled poacher's den.

LEVEL 1 (KNOWLEDGE)

o Where are Tim and Lisa visiting?

o What do Ngoya and Tumba do?

o Who are Kabedi and Tumba?

o What is the Legend of the Six-Eyed Monster?

LEVEL 2 (COMPREHENSION)

o Explain how Tim got separated from the group.

o Summarize how poachers work.

o What is a "savanna" like?

o Describe the activities going on in the village market.

LEVEL 3 (APPLICATION)

o Have you see spectacular wild animals from Africa in a zoo? Tell what they were like.

o Have you ever lived with a host family in a foreign country, or wished you could? Tell what such an experience could teach a person.

o Do you have a brother or sister? Who's the boss?

LEVEL 4 (ANALYSIS)

o Compare the brother-sister relationship of Tim and Lisa to that of Kabedi and Tumba.

o How are the boys alike?

o How are the girls alike?

o Why can poachers get away with poaching so easily?

o Compare the village and home of Kabedi and Tumba to your home and town.

o Compare Ngoya and Miteo to your own parents.

LEVEL 5 (SYNTHESIS)

o Would an established on-site action group to prevent poaching have made a difference in Tim's initial observation?

o Name the large animals that Tim was expecting to see.

o If you stumbled upon the poacher's den, what would you do next?

o If the poacher discovered you snooping around his place, what would you say and do?

o If you were at a posh restaurant and the waiter told you that the antelope meat on the menu was provided by a well-paid poacher, what would you do?

o Would you eat everything your hosts offered you? Explain.

LEVEL 6 (EVALUATION)

o Judge the value of an Okapi Club to a region.

o What is the major advantage of having children as well as adults as members in the Okapi Club?

o What legal penalty should poachers suffer?

o Who is more emotional, Tim or Lisa?

o Is it necessary to preserve Africa's large, wild animals?

o If Tim and Lisa were allergic to pollen, mold and spores, how would the story change?

Anastasia, Ask Your Analyst

by Lois Lowry

Anastasia, a thirteen-year old, is having difficulty dealing with her mother. Anastasia believes that a psychiatrist might be the answer. There are amusing dialogs and interactions between mother and daughter and baby brother, a "fudge-like" little "wiz." Anastasia matures through the events of everyday life.

LEVEL 1 (KNOWLEDGE)

○ What was Anastasia's little brother's name?

○ What grade was Anastasia in?

○ Name some of Anastasia's gerbils.

○ Who came to Anastasia's house and caused all kinds of problems?

○ To whom did Anastasia talk about her problems?

LEVEL 2 (COMPREHENSION)

○ Describe Mrs. Krupnik's feelings about gerbils.

○ Explain why Anastasia wanted to see a psychiatrist.

○ Describe some things Mrs. Krupnik did which annoyed Anastasia.

○ Tell what happened to Anastasia's Science Project.

LEVEL 3 (APPLICATION)

○ Have you experienced difficulty in communicating with your parents? Explain.

○ How would your parents react to eleven gerbils?

o Did you ever feel that you had emotional problems? Explain.

o Have you had problems that just seem to work themselves out?

LEVEL 4 (ANALYSIS)

o Compare Sam to your little brother or sister.

o Compare Anastasia's Science Project to a project that you had to do for school.

o Analyze Anastasia's feelings about wanting to see a psychiatrist.

o Could Mrs. Krupnik have a phobia about gerbils? Explain.

o What was the relationship between Mr. and Mrs. Krupnik?

o Analyze Anastasia's feelings when Mr. Krupnik took the gerbils away.

LEVEL 5 (SYNTHESIS)

o Suppose the gerbils had multiplied to 30 or 40. How would Anastasia have handled that many?

o Suppose the Krupnik's had a pet cat. What would have happened when the gerbils were loose?

o How could Anastasia have improved her relationship with her mother? Explain.

o Think of a few science projects you could do with gerbils.

o Describe Anastasia's next pet.

o If Anastasia met a real psychiatrist in the story, what would she have said about her mother?

LEVEL 6 (EVALUATION)

○ Was Anastasia being reasonable about her mother's behavior? Explain.

○ Do you think Anastasia really needed psychiatric help? Why?

○ How would you evaluate Anastasia's Science Project?

○ Which event in the story gave you a good indication of Anastasia's personality?

○ Judge Mrs. Krupnik as a mother.

○ Predict what the relationship will be like between Anastasia and her mother in the future.

Introducing: Milton S. Tipple

by Glenda Fountain King

Milton is a preteen who is on the edge of stepping out of childhood. His escapades are funny. He is self-absorbed and in constant motion, concerned with appearances and posturing to act older. In spite of his antics, his family remains loving and his friends true.

LEVEL 1 (KNOWLEDGE)

o How old is Milton?

o Who are Milton's friends?

o Who are in Milton's family.

o What does Milton do on Saturday mornings?

LEVEL 2 (COMPREHENSION)

o Why doesn't Milton tell his friends that he watches cartoons on Saturday morning?

o Why is Milton jealous of Sam?

o What does Milton think he's proving by shaving his head?

o Why is Milton jealous of his baby sister?

LEVEL 3 (APPLICATION)

o Have you ever tried to impress your friends by exaggerating the truth? Explain.

o Have you ever lied to impress a friend? Explain.

o Describe the interior of your bedroom. Is it like Milton's?

o What does making a fashion statement have to do with maturity?

LEVEL 4 (ANALYSIS)

o How is Milton like an average pre-teen?

o Compare Milton to a boy you know.

o Why did Milton neglect to tell his parents about Open School Night?

o What did Milton learn from his "mooning" experience?

o Analyze Sam's character. How does he come through for Milton?

o Which actions of Milton's can you identify with?

LEVEL 5 (SYNTHESIS)

o If Milton had known his grandmother was in the car behind the bus, would his actions have been different?

o If Milton's parents had known about Open School Night, what would change in the story?

o List the lies and half-truths Milton told. What else could you add to this list from the files of your own friends?

o If Milton's baby sister could speak, what would she tell Milton?

o If you were Milton's teacher, what would you tell his parents?

o Think of another antic that would fit Milton's personality.

LEVEL 6 (EVALUATION)

o Judge Milton's character.

o Is Milton's mother too picky about his neatness?

o Does Milton show signs of growing up? Explain.

o Judge how Milton's friends treat him.

o Judge how Milton's parents treat him.

o Is Sam a good brother?

Bridge To Terabithia

by Katherine Paterson

Jess Aarons had to be the fastest runner at Lark Creek Elementary School, the best, but when he was challenged by Leslie Burke, a girl, that was just the beginning of a new season in Jess's life. Somewhat to Jess's surprise, he and Leslie became friends, and the worlds of imagination and learning that she opened to him changed him forever.

LEVEL 1 (KNOWLEDGE)

○ Where did Jess and Leslie live?

○ What was the name of their secret kingdom in the woods?

○ What gift did Jess give Leslie?

○ What happened to Leslie while Jess was in Washington?

LEVEL 2 (COMPREHENSION)

○ Describe Jess's attitude about running before losing to Leslie.

○ Describe the secret kingdom of Terabithia.

○ Tell what Leslie and Jess liked to talk about while at Terabithia.

○ Describe what Leslie taught Jess about life.

LEVEL 3 (APPLICATION)

○ Do you have a good friend of the opposite sex? Explain.

○ Do you know someone like Leslie who has a great imagination?

○ Have you ever visited a farm? If yes, describe it.

○ How would you have handled Leslie's death?

LEVEL 4 (ANALYSIS)

○ Analyze the relationship between Jess and Leslie.

○ Compare their relationship to a relationship you have with a friend.

○ Decide whether Jess and Leslie's relationship was unusual.

○ What type of person was Jess? Explain.

○ How would you describe the life Jess lived on the farm?

○ Analyze Jess's reaction and coping with the unexpected tragedy.

LEVEL 5 (SYNTHESIS)

○ If Leslie hadn't beaten Jess in the race, would that have changed the story?

○ Suppose other students had learned about Terabithia. How would they have reacted?

○ Where would you build a secret kingdom?

○ With whom would you want to share a secret kingdom?

○ Create a different ending to the story.

○ Name three personal qualities about Leslie that Jess will always remember.

LEVEL 6 (EVALUATION)

○ What did you learn from this story?

○ Was Jess a typical fifth grader?

○ How was Leslie different from most fifth grade girls?

○ Should Leslie and Jess have had a secret kingdom out in the woods? Why?

○ Why should other children read this story?

○ What adult would you want to read this story?

The Great Gilly Hopkins

by Katherine Paterson

At eleven, Gilly is nobody's real kid. If only she could find her beautiful mother, Courtney, and live with her instead of in the ugly foster home where she has just been placed. Gutsy Gilly is both poignant and comic as, behind her best barracuda smile, she schemes against them and everyone else who tries to be friendly. The reader will cheer for her as she copes with the longings and terrors of always being a foster child.

LEVEL 1 (KNOWLEDGE)

○ What was Gilly's foster mother's name?

○ Who else lived in the Trotter house?

○ Where did Gilly move to after leaving Thompson Park?

○ When did Gilly's mother finally come home to see her daughter?

LEVEL 2 (COMPREHENSION)

○ Describe Gilly's foster mother, Mrs. Trotter.

○ Explain the difficulties Gilly had living in the Trotter house.

○ How did Gilly plan to go and visit her mother?

○ Describe how Gilly finally met her real mother.

LEVEL 3 (APPLICATION)

○ Could you have lived in the Trotter house? Why?

○ What would be the most difficult thing for you to accept if you had to live in a foster home?

○ What do you like about Gilly? Explain.

○ Would Gilly be happy living with your family? Why?

LEVEL 4 (ANALYSIS)

○ Which event in the story clearly demonstrated the difficulties of being a foster child?

○ What type of foster mother was Mrs. Trotter?

○ Why do you think Mrs. Trotter wanted to be a foster mother?

○ Analyze the Trotter house in terms of its being an acceptable home for Gilly.

○ What was Gilly's main complaint about being in a foster home?

○ How would you analyze Gilly's feelings about being on her grandmother's farm?

LEVEL 5 (SYNTHESIS)

○ Why do you feel that Gilly will become a successful, productive adult?

○ What would you like to say to Gilly if you could meet her?

○ Describe a perfect vacation for Gilly.

○ What happened to Gilly's real father?

○ Create a new ending to the story.

○ Describe what Gilly would like best about the things you do in your life.

LEVEL 6 (EVALUATION)

○ Judge the quality of the Trotter house in terms of it being a foster home.

o Evaluate Gilly's efforts in trying to find her mother.

o Judge Gilly's mother's reasons for not wanting her daughter all those years.

o What makes the story valuable to you as a person? Explain.

o Predict whether Gilly will ever have a successful relationship with her mother.

o What did this story teach you about the life of a foster child?

Kid Power

by Susan Beth Pfeffer

When Janie Golden's mom was laid off from her job, the family had to forego luxuries—such as the ten speed bikes Janie and Carol wanted. And that's how "Kid Power" started.

LEVEL 1 (KNOWLEDGE)

○ What was Janie's sister's name?

○ Who gave Janie her first job?

○ Which job gave Janie the most difficulty?

○ Who worked for Janie in her Kid Power Agency?

LEVEL 2 (COMPREHENSION)

○ Describe Janie's first paying job.

○ Name the other jobs Janie got from Kid Power.

○ Who did Janie really help in the story?

○ Describe what Janie did to learn more about handling money.

LEVEL 3 (APPLICATION)

○ Have you ever worked for money? Explain.

○ What types of jobs could your mom and dad give to someone like Janie?

○ Would you want to work for Janie? Why?

○ Do you know anyone who is like Janie Golden? Explain.

LEVEL 4 (ANALYSIS)

○ Which job was Janie's most difficult?

○ Which job should Janie have received more money for?

○ Which event in the story really demonstrated Janie's ability?

○ Compare Janie to someone (a friend) you know who works for money.

○ What personal quality helps make Janie so successful in Kid Power?

○ Analyze Janie's sister's reaction to all the success she achieved through Kid Power.

LEVEL 5 (SYNTHESIS)

○ Think of another name for Janie's business.

○ Name other jobs Janie could have done in her community.

○ Think of some newspaper headlines explaining Janie's Kid Power.

○ Describe Kid Power when Janie is fifteen years old.

○ Tell how you would start your own Kid Power Company.

○ What type of career might Janie find herself in as an adult?

LEVEL 6 (EVALUATION)

○ Should someone as young as Janie earn money through a Kid Power Agency? Why?

○ Evaluate the reasons Janie started Kid Power.

○ Judge Janie's success with Kid Power.

○ Decide whether Janie received fair wages for her work.

○ How much money could Janie earn in one year?

○ Predict whether Janie will continue with Kid Power as she grows up.

The Westing Game

by Ellen Raskin

Sixteen people were invited to the reading of the very strange will of the very rich Samuel W. Westing. They could become millionaires depending on how they played the game. The Westing game was tricky and dangerous, but the heirs played on, through blizzards and burglaries and bombs bursting in air. And one of them won!

LEVEL 1 (KNOWLEDGE)

○ **Who was Samuel W. Westing?**

○ How did Samuel W. Westing really die?

○ Who in the story was Mr. Westing's wife?

○ How much was Mr. Westing's will worth?

LEVEL 2 (COMPREHENSION)

○ Describe how the sixteen people received their clues.

○ Explain what the clues were like.

○ Explain how the people were asked for their answers to the Westing game.

○ Tell how and who won the Westing game.

LEVEL 3 (APPLICATION)

○ Have you ever played a commercial game where you had to solve the murder? Explain.

○ Do you know of any unsolved cases where there are only clues and no real solutions? Explain.

○ Would you have wanted to be one of the sixteen heirs? Why?

○ Can you name some commercially sold games that are like the Westing Game?

LEVEL 4 (ANALYSIS)

○ Compare Samuel Westing to some rich, eccentric millionaire you have heard about.

○ When in the story did you have an idea about how Mr. Westing died?

○ Analyze the clues given to the sixteen people. Compare these clues to real life clues found in an actual investigation.

○ Early in the story, who did you think might be accused of Mr. Westing's death?

○ Compare the Westing Game to the commercial game "Clue."

○ Under the circumstances, how would you classify the actions and behavior of the heirs during the Westing Game?

LEVEL 5 (SYNTHESIS)

○ Tell how you really believe Samuel Westing died.

○ How could you improve, make better, the Westing Game?

○ What type of personality was missing from the sixteen heirs? Explain.

○ Create a different outcome to the Westing Game.

○ Name an adult that you know that would absolutely love to have been involved in the Westing Game.

○ Make up a new name for the Westing Game.

LEVEL 6 (EVALUATION)

○ Judge whether the Westing Game could ever really take place. Why?

○ What aspect of the Westing Game did you mostly dislike? Why?

○ How could the Westing Game have been improved? Explain.

○ Evaluate Samuel Westing's motives for creating the Westing Game.

○ Why would adults enjoy reading the Westing Game?

○ Evaluate the outcome of the Westing Game.

Grandfather Webster's Strange Will

by Sherbrooke Rogers

A world-famous mystery writer leaves a hidden treasure to his four grandchildren in his will. Each youngster receives several clues to the mystery that must be solved by the end of the summer. The four cousins who have always been in competition with one another now must join forces to solve the mystery.

LEVEL 1 (KNOWLEDGE)

o Who was J. J. Webster?

o Who is telling the story?

o Describe Joanne, Ellie and Glenn.

o How old must the children be before they may use their money?

LEVEL 2 (COMPREHENSION)

o Explain what a *will* is?

o How did grandfather amass the collections for the youngsters?

o Explain why Ellie got some pieces of grandmother's jewelry.

o What kinds of dolls would have been in Joanne's collection?

LEVEL 3 (APPLICATION)

o Have you, or someone you know, ever been left anything in a will?

o Have you ever known a person who traveled a lot? What made him or her interesting?

o How would you feel about inheriting $25,000 for your future use?

LEVEL 4 (ANALYSIS)

o Analyze grandfather's reason for giving each youngster only a part of the puzzle's clues.

o What was grandfather thinking about as he traveled around the world?

o Is it probable that grandfather spoke more than one language?

o Compare the feelings of the oldest and youngest grandchild about their inheritance.

o Why did the riddle of the will have to be solved by summer's end?

o Was grandfather a lonely man?

LEVEL 5 (SYNTHESIS)

o How would the story change if grandfather left only money?

o What would happen if the cousins did not share their clues?

o If grandfather were an artist instead of an author, how would his will be different? Explain.

o Would the story work as well if grandfather wrote romance novels?

o If the story were set in the 1890's, what would be different?

o If there were no female grandchildren, what would happen to grandmother's jewelry?

LEVEL 6 (EVALUATION)

o List grandfather's good characteristics.

o What was the most valuable part of grandfather's bequest to each youngster?

o Explain the value of owning the royalty rights to a book that will probably be a best seller.

o How is grandfather's will like one of his novels?

o What evidence shows that grandfather loved each grandchild as an individual.

o Which of the grandchildren was most touched by grandfather's bequest?

How To Eat Fried Worms

by Thomas Rockwell

By way of a bet, Billy gets into the uncomfortable position of having to eat fifteen worms. The worms are readily supplied by his opponent, and Billy has a free choice of condiments, from peanut butter to horse radish.

LEVEL 1 (KNOWLEDGE)

○ With whom did Billy make the bet?

○ How many worms did Billy have to eat?

○ How much money did Billy win for eating the fifteen worms?

○ How did Billy get the final fifteenth worm?

LEVEL 2 (COMPREHENSION)

○ Describe how the worms were prepared and served to Billy.

○ How did Billy's friends try to trick him?

○ Explain how Billy's parents reacted when they found out about the worm eating.

○ Describe how Billy was able to get and eat the fifteenth worm.

LEVEL 3 (APPLICATION)

○ Have you ever eaten an insect? Explain.

○ Have you ever been challenged to eat something other than food?

○ How would your parents have reacted if they learned that you had eaten worms?

○ Who do you know that might eat a worm on a bet?

LEVEL 4 (ANALYSIS)

○ What was the most difficult thing about eating worms for Billy?

○ Which of the tricks Billy's friends played on him was the most unfair?

○ Why would anyone want to eat worms?

○ Analyze Billy's worm eating methods and choice of condiments.

○ How would you classify Billy's parents' reaction to learning about the worm eating?

○ How would you classify Billy's personality?

LEVEL 5 (SYNTHESIS)

○ Describe what the worms tasted like.

○ What other insects could Billy have eaten instead of worms?

○ Name some other condiments which could have helped Billy consume the worms.

○ Describe a worm eating contest. Tell how you would have such an event.

○ Describe what your parents would say to you if you had eaten fifteen worms.

○ Think of some other "How To Eat" books the author Thomas Rockwell could write for children.

LEVEL 6 (EVALUATION)

○ Judge whether any of your friends could be tempted into eating worms.

136

○ Which would taste the worst—a worm or a large bug? Why?

○ How many young children do you think have eaten worms?

○ What could happen to someone if they were to eat fifteen worms?

○ Why is this story so enjoyed by children?

○ Why did Billy have to eat fifteen worms—why couldn't he have eaten just one?

Count The Stars Through The Cracks

by Billie Hotaling

A brother and sister set out with their mother to escape from the plantation in the south where they are slaves. The destination is Canada, but the mother dies early in the journey. The two siblings traverse the Underground Railroad to Ohio, where nine-year-old Susu breaks her leg. They stay with a free black family until her leg is healed, and fifteen-year-old Jute gets a salary working for the husband on his mill. When they are ready to move north again, Civil War breaks out. The youngsters are free in Ohio!

LEVEL 1 (KNOWLEDGE)

o Where are Jute and Susu heading?

o What happens on the day they are ready to leave Ohio?

o What accident forces them to stay in Ohio?

o When does the story take place?

LEVEL 2 (COMPREHENSION)

o Explain how the Underground Railroad worked.

o Describe Susu's disguise.

o Tell how Jute reacted to getting paid for his work.

o Describe how Jute and Susu escaped in the sheep railroad car.

LEVEL 3 (APPLICATION)

o Do you know anyone who has escaped from oppression? Explain.

o Have you ever had to delay your plans because of a brother or sister? Explain.

o If you were Jute and now free with money in your pocket, what would you do with it?

o What does being able to read mean to you? To Susu?

LEVEL 4 (ANALYSIS)

o Analyze the relationship between Jute and Susu.

o Compare Jute to one of your friends who has a will to win.

o Analyze Susu's feelings towards Mrs. Geer.

o How would you describe Mr. Geer?

o Compare Doctor Sammison to your family doctor.

o Analyze Jute's feelings when Susu broke her leg.

LEVEL 5 (SYNTHESIS)

o What might have happened if Susu didn't break her leg?

o How would the story be different if the Civil War had not begun?

o How will Susu's and Jute's expectations for their children differ from the expectations their parents had for them?

o Create a front page headline for the day Susu and Jute arrive in Xenia to buy railroad tickets to Canada.

o Describe how the free black family's life will change once their mill is up and running.

o What qualities about Jute will Susu always remember?

LEVEL 6 (EVALUATION)

o Why would Jute have trouble trusting white people?

o Who helped slaves escape via the Underground Railroad?

o Evaluate the importance of Susu's learning to read.

o How is pride in oneself a positive motivation?

o Why was helping slaves escape dangerous for white sympathizers?

o What could Jute buy with the money he saved instead of railroad tickets.

The Little Prince

by Antoine de Saint-Exupery

"Six years ago," writes Antione de Saint-Exupery, "I made a forced landing in the Sahara. Thus it was there that I met the Little Prince, whose strange history I learned, bit by bit, in the days that followed."

LEVEL 1 (KNOWLEDGE)

○ What did the Little Prince ask the man to draw?

○ What did the Little Prince own?

○ Who told the Little Prince the secret of what is really important in life?

○ Who did the Little Prince meet as he traveled Earth?

LEVEL 2 (COMPREHENSION)

○ Describe how the Little Prince felt about his tiny planet.

○ Describe what annoyed the man about the Little Prince.

○ Explain what the Little Prince learned as he journeyed Earth.

○ Describe how the man felt when the Little Prince disappeared at the end of the story.

LEVEL 3 (APPLICATION)

○ Do you know anyone who is like the Little Prince? Explain.

○ What message does the story of the Little Prince give you? Explain.

○ Could you have done anything to help the Little Prince? What?

o What would your parents have wanted to say to the Little Prince?

LEVEL 4 (ANALYSIS)

o Why was the Little Prince so involved with his flower?

o Analyze the Little Prince's planet.

o To whom did the Little Prince give a real negative picture of life?

o Who gave the Little Prince the most encouragement? Why?

o How did inordinate pride hurt the Little Prince?

o Compare the Little Prince with E.T.

LEVEL 5 (SYNTHESIS)

o Who else would you have wanted the Little Prince to meet during his visit on Earth?

o Make up a nickname for the Little Prince.

o When will the Little Prince return to Earth?

o Think of some things to add to the Little Prince's planet?

o Describe what kind of job the Little Prince might be suited for on Earth.

o What do you think is the Little Prince's favorite color? Why?

LEVEL 6 (EVALUATION)

o Judge why the man felt sorry for the Little Prince.

o How could the Little Prince have helped the man?

○ Evaluate what the Fox said to the Little Prince "What is essential is invisible to the eye."

○ What could the Little Prince learn from living with you and your family?

○ What three things did the story about the Little Prince teach you?

○ Why should other students read the Little Prince?

Black Beauty

by Anna Sewell

A sensitive, warm autobiography of a horse. The life of Black Beauty is told in a manner that captures the relationships between horses and their masters.

LEVEL 1 (KNOWLEDGE)

○ Where was Black Beauty born?

○ Who was Black Beauty's first master?

○ Who became Black Beauty's closest horse friend?

○ When did Black Beauty become weak and sick?

LEVEL 2 (COMPREHENSION)

○ Describe Black Beauty's early days at Birtwick Park.

○ Describe Black Beauty's temperament as a horse.

○ Tell what Black Beauty enjoyed.

○ Explain how Black Beauty became weak and sick.

LEVEL 3 (APPLICATION)

○ Have you ever owned a horse? Explain.

○ Describe any experiences you have had with horses.

○ Have you ever wondered whether animals have feelings like human beings? Explain.

○ What type of master would you have been for Black Beauty? Explain.

LEVEL 4 (ANALYSIS)

○ Why was Black Beauty considered to be a real fine horse?

○ Which event in the story demonstrated Black Beauty's caring attitude?

○ Why did Ginger have such a fiery temper?

○ Which activities did Black Beauty enjoy doing the most?

○ Why is taking care of a horse a demanding job?

○ Why was Black Beauty such a positive influence on Ginger?

LEVEL 5 (SYNTHESIS)

○ Why would Black Beauty like you and your family?

○ Where would you like to take Black Beauty if he were yours?

○ Could Black Beauty have been a race horse? Why?

○ How could Black Beauty have shown his displeasure for an inhuman, insensitive master?

○ If you could have spent a weekend with Black Beauty, what kinds of things would you have done with him?

○ Why didn't Black Beauty ever have any famous children?

LEVEL 6 (EVALUATION)

○ Judge which master was Black Beauty's favorite.

○ What is the most difficult aspect of caring for a horse?

○ Why has Black Beauty remained a children's classic for decades?

○ What does this story teach you? Explain.

○ How does Black Beauty help you in thinking about other animals?

The Sign Of The Beaver

by Elizabeth George Speare

Although he faced his responsibility bravely, thirteen year old Matt was more than a little apprehensive when his father left him alone to guard their newly built cabin in the wilderness. After meeting a resourceful Indian boy, Matt began to discover new ways to survive in the forest.

LEVEL 1 (KNOWLEDGE)

○ Where did Matt's family own a log cabin?

○ What was the Indian boy's name?

○ What animals did the Indian boy and Matt hunt?

○ When did Matt's family finally return to the cabin?

○ What year did this story take place?

LEVEL 2 (COMPREHENSION)

○ Describe the setting where Matt lived?

○ Tell how the stranger stole Matt's father's gun.

○ Tell how Saknis first met Matt and what he did for Matt.

○ Describe how Matt survived the beginning of winter.

LEVEL 3 (APPLICATION)

○ What aspect of Matt's adventure would you have had difficulty with? Explain.

○ Have you ever spent the night camping out in the woods? What was it like?

○ What lessons did you learn from this story?

o What would you have wanted to do if you were Matt in the story? Explain.

LEVEL 4 (ANALYSIS)

o Why was getting food to eat a difficult challenge for Matt?

o What was the Indian's attitude about the white settlers?

o Compare Matt's attitude about life to the Indian boy's attitude about life.

o Which event in the story really made you aware of Matt's responsibilities?

o What types of gestures or communications worked well for Matt in gaining the confidence of his Indian friends?

o Which event in the story would have terrified you the most?

LEVEL 5 (SYNTHESIS)

o Suppose Ben wanted to spend several weeks living in Matt's cabin. How would that have changed the story?

o What if Matt had gotten real sick and needed a doctor—what might have happened?

o Why didn't Matt ever try to go back to Massachusetts to find his Pa?

o Describe all the different kinds of food Matt ate during the months he was alone.

o How could Matt have gotten a message to his Pa?

o How much wood did Matt have to burn in a day to keep his cabin warm?

LEVEL 6 (EVALUATION)

○ Decide how long Matt would have waited for his Pa before trying to contact him back in Massachusetts.

○ Judge the most difficult responsibility Matt had.

○ Why was Matt successful in making friends with the Indians? Explain.

○ Judge why Saknis was so helpful and nice to Matt.

○ Predict what would have happened to Matt if some white traders had angered Saknis's clan.

○ Predict how Matt and his family will get along with the Indians in the future.

The Pearl

by John Steinbeck

"In the town they tell the story of the great pearl—how it was found and how it was lost again. They tell of Kino, the fisherman, and of his wife, Juana, and of the baby, Coyotito." They talk of the excitement and potential wealth from the pearl and how the images turned to evil and despair.

LEVEL 1 (KNOWLEDGE)

○ Who were the members of the family in the story?

○ Who found the pearl?

○ How much was Kino offered for the pearl?

○ What happened to the baby Coyotito at the end of the story?

LEVEL 2 (COMPREHENSION)

○ Describe where Kino, Juana, and Coyotito lived.

○ Explain how Kino found the pearl.

○ Tell what the traders said to Kino about the pearl's value.

○ Describe the family's escape and tragedy.

LEVEL 3 (APPLICATION)

○ What do you have that is of great value to you and your family? Explain.

○ Why can a found treasure become a burden?

○ What do you have that someone might want to steal?

○ What would you have done with the pearl? Explain.

LEVEL 4 (ANALYSIS)

○ Describe the relationship between Kino and Juana.

○ What were Kino's feelings when the doctor first refused to treat Coyotito?

○ Analyze the motives of the traders who offered Kino such low prices for the pearl.

○ Why were there so many people interested in stealing this pearl?

○ Analyze Kino's attitude and feelings when he threw the pearl back into the sea.

○ Why did Kino feel the pearl was a curse to him?

LEVEL 5 (SYNTHESIS)

○ Suppose Kino received great wealth from the pearl. How might that have changed his life?

○ Describe in detail the "Pearl of the World."

○ Could Kino have prevented the tragedies in the story?

○ Create a new title for this tale.

○ Describe how the pearl is found in the future.

○ Tell how the story would be different if the pearl was found today.

LEVEL 6 (EVALUATION)

○ Evaluate the manner in which Kino acted after he found the pearl.

○ Judge Kino's actions when he killed the man trying to steal his pearl.

150

○ Judge the value of the pearl. What do you think it was worth?

○ Were other great pearls found during that time?

○ Judge Kino's actions when he threw the pearl back into the sea.

○ Why has this story remained a classic in children's literature?

The Lady Or The Tiger

by Frank Stockton

A classic story of a semi-barbaric King whose policy of justice was to have the accused walk into the arena and select his/her own fate by deciding which door to enter. The one door had a vicious tiger behind it, while the other door had a beautiful young lady waiting to be married. The story is of a young man who must make this decision.

LEVEL 1 (KNOWLEDGE)

○ Where did the King hold trial?

○ Who attended the King's trials?

○ What was the young man accused of by the King?

○ What was behind the two doors in the arena?

LEVEL 2 (COMPREHENSION)

○ Describe what the King's amphitheater was like.

○ Explain the King's system of justice.

○ Tell what the public thought of the King's justice system.

○ Tell how the Princess signaled her lover while he stood in the King's arena.

LEVEL 3 (APPLICATION)

○ What other leaders in history had similar barbaric policies concerning justice?

○ Where do you hear, today, the saying "it's your choice"?

○ How would you feel about making the choice between the two doors? Explain.

○ Have you ever had to make a very difficult choice? Explain.

LEVEL 4 (ANALYSIS)

○ Analyze the relationship between the Princess and the young man in the story.

○ Why did the public enjoy the King's system of justice? Explain.

○ How do you think the accused would make the final choice between the two doors? Explain.

○ Analyze the Princess's feelings as she signaled to her young lover in the King's arena.

○ Describe the relationship between the King and his daughter the Princess.

○ Analyze one's feelings having selected the door where the young lady stood.

LEVEL 5 (SYNTHESIS)

○ Make up a third door which could be used by the King.

○ Describe the day in which the King was put into the arena of justice.

○ Explain how there could be a tiger behind each door.

○ Think of some ways of escaping from the tiger had you selected that door.

○ Give the King's system of justice a name.

○ Tell about the results of the first one hundred people who were put into the King's arena of justice.

LEVEL 6 (EVALUATION)

○ Why would the King be so barbaric in his system of justice? Explain.

o Evaluate the young man's crime.

o Judge whether the King had second thoughts about sending the young man into the arena.

o How many years do you think that type of justice system lasted?

o Which door did the Princess signal for her lover to enter? Explain.

o Evaluate the Princess's feelings once her lover made his door selection and accepted the consequences.

The Cay

by Theodore Taylor

An exciting story about a young boy named Phillip who was blinded during a war time explosion and was led to safety by an old black man named Timothy. For months they lived on a small island waiting to be rescued. A very moving adventure about their struggle for survival.

LEVEL 1 (KNOWLEDGE)

○ What happened to Phillip during the sinking of the *Hato?*

○ Who saved Phillip's life?

○ What did Phillip and Timothy eat on the Cay?

○ What happened to Timothy after the big storm on the Cay?

LEVEL 2 (COMPREHENSION)

○ Describe how the *Hato* was sunk.

○ Explain how Timothy saved Phillip's life.

○ Describe how Phillip and Timothy survived in the Cay.

○ Tell how Phillip kept himself alive after Timothy died.

LEVEL 3 (APPLICATION)

○ What would have been the hardest aspect of Phillip's struggle for survival for you? Explain.

○ Have you ever thought about being stranded on an island? Explain.

○ What impressed you the most about Phillip? Explain.

○ Have you ever met a person who had the courage Timothy had in the story? Explain.

LEVEL 4 (ANALYSIS)

○ Why did Phillip and Timothy have some difficulty getting along at first?

○ Which event in the story demonstrated just how brave Phillip was?

○ Compare Phillip's struggle to survive with another survival story you know about.

○ How would you describe Timothy?

○ Why did it take so long for Phillip to be found?

○ Compare this story with another human interest story.

LEVEL 5 (SYNTHESIS)

○ Suppose Phillip wasn't rescued shortly after Timothy's death. How long could be have survived?

○ Describe what it must have been like to be blind and all alone on the Cay.

○ What dangers could Timothy and Phillip have encountered on the Cay?

○ Why didn't Timothy and Phillip build a raft and sail from the island?

○ What might have Phillip's parents done in their search for their son?

○ Think of another character who could have fit into the story.

LEVEL 6 (EVALUATION)

○ Judge whether it would be possible to survive on an island alone and blinded.

○ Did Phillip and Timothy do all that was possible to increase their chances of being rescued.

○ Decide whether you could have survived on the island alone and blinded.

○ What would have been the most difficult part in struggling to survive on an island such as the Cay?

○ Predict whether Phillip will ever go back to visit the Cay.

Mickie

by Edith Unnerstad

When this notice (below) appears in a Stockholm newspaper one morning, no one suspects that the mysterious sounding "Madame Charite" is really an eleven year old girl. Even Mickie Fikberg's parents and her cousin Mona, who are used to Mickie's sometimes complicated schemes, don't guess—at first.

Young lady, intending to practice charity, wishes to make the acquaintance of genuinely needy persons, preferably families with many children. Address communications to Madame Charite, Aalsten Post Office.

LEVEL 1 (KNOWLEDGE)

○ Where did Mickie live?

○ Where did Mickie's Uncle Martin have to go to?

○ Who helped Mickie with her great scheme?

○ What was Uncle Martin's gift to Mickie?

LEVEL 2 (COMPREHENSION)

○ Describe Mickie's life in Stockholm.

○ Tell about the response Mickie received as a result of her newspaper ad.

○ Describe Mickie's relationship with Uncle Martin.

○ Explain what Mickie learned most from her great scheme.

LEVEL 3 (APPLICATION)

○ Why would Mickie be a neat friend to have?

158

○ How could you have helped Mickie in the story? Explain.

○ Why would Mickie be nice to have as a sister?

○ Do you have an uncle like Uncle Martin? Explain.

LEVEL 4 (ANALYSIS)

○ Analyze Mickie's risk-taking behavior.

○ Which event in the story, demonstrated Mickie's true personality?

○ Why did Mickie want to help other people?

○ What in the story made you really like Mickie as a person? Be specific.

○ Compare Mickie to an eleven year old girl you know real well.

○ Compare one of Mickie's schemes to a scheme you have gotten involved in.

LEVEL 5 (SYNTHESIS)

○ Think of a new scheme that Mickie would really enjoy doing.

○ What new hobbies would Mickie like to get involved in?

○ Name three places in your community Mickie would enjoy visiting.

○ Change one event in the story which would have a definite impact on the outcome of the story.

○ What type of career will Mickie do well in when she is an adult?

○ If Mickie could have wished for a "miracle" in the story, what would it have been?

LEVEL 6 (EVALUATION)

○ Why should young people read *Mickie*? Explain.

○ What was Mickie's biggest obstacle in the story? Explain.

○ Evaluate the relationship Mickie had with her parents.

○ Name three things that you learned from Mickie's adventures.

○ Think of something you would have like to have added to the story—a situation, a character, an event, etc.

○ Predict what kinds of schemes Mickie might get herself into in the future.

The Inexperienced Ghost

by H. G. Wells

H. G. Wells, the first modern writer to combine the world of the supernatural with twentieth-century science fiction, occasionally ventured into the realm of the fanciful. In this work, he gives us a delightful tale of a phantom who is inexperienced!

LEVEL 1 (KNOWLEDGE)

○ Where did Clayton discover the ghost?

○ To whom was Clayton telling his ghost story?

○ What had happened to the inexperienced ghost in real life?

○ What happened to Clayton at the end of the story?

LEVEL 2 (COMPREHENSION)

○ Describe what the ghost looked like.

○ Explain why the ghost was inexperienced.

○ Tell why the ghost was so unhappy.

○ Describe what the ghost did before finally disappearing.

LEVEL 3 (APPLICATION)

○ Why are people so interested in ghost stories?

○ What cartoons and movies have been made about ghosts?

○ Have you ever dreamed about a ghost? If yes, explain.

○ Do you know anyone who believes in ghosts? Explain.

LEVEL 4 (ANALYSIS)

○ Why did Clayton's friends listen to his ghost story?

- Why did Clayton's ghost story appear real?

- Analyze the ghost's characteristics which made it inexperienced.

- Which event in the story made it seem like a real story?

- What caused Clayton to die at the end of the story?

- Compare this ghost story to another ghost story you are familiar with.

LEVEL 5 (SYNTHESIS)

- Suppose this inexperienced ghost were to visit you. How would you have treated it?

- When did people first begin thinking about ghosts?

- Tell a ghost story.

- Describe where ghosts live.

- How would an experienced ghost have acted in Clayton's club?

- Tell about three things ghosts like to do.

LEVEL 6 (EVALUATION)

- Judge the quality of Clayton's ghost story.

- What made the story so believable?

- Where do most ghost stories take place?

- Predict what would happen if a real ghost was seen.

- Why are ghosts so interesting?

- Do you think you will ever see a ghost? Why?

APPENDIX 1
Bloom's Taxonomy of Educational Objectives

KNOWLEDGE	SKILLS
1. Knowledge of specifics	*define, recognize*
knowledge of terminology	*recall*
knowledge of specific facts	*identify, label*
2. Knowledge of Ways of Dealing With Specifics	*understand*
knowledge of conventions	*examine*
knowledge of trends and sequences	*show*
knowledge of classifications and categories	*collect*
knowledge of criteria	
knowledge of methodology	
3. Knowledge of Universals & Abstractions in a Field	
knowledge of principles and generalizations	
knowledge of theories and structures	

COMPREHENSION

1. Translation	*translate, interpret*
2. Interpretation	*predict, summarize*
3. Extrapolation	*describe, explain*

APPLICATION   *apply, solve*

1. Use Abstractions in Specific & Concrete Situations	*experiment, show*

ANALYSIS   *connect, classify*

1. Analysis of Elements	*differentiate, relate*
2. Analysis of Relationships	*classify, arrange*
3. Analysis of Organizational Principles	*group, compare*

SYNTHESIS   *imagine*

1. Production of a Unique Communication	*design, redesign*
2. Production of a Plan for Operation	*combine, compose*
3. Derivation of a Set of Abstract Relations	*construct, translate*

EVALUATION

1. Judgments in Terms of Internal Evidence.	*interpret, judge*
2. Judgments in Terms of External Evidence.	*criticize, decide*

APPENDIX ll

Verbs for Curriculum Development

Identification	Processes		
Model	Verb Delineation		

Taxonomy			
Knowledge	explain	relate	design
	show	code	interpret
Comprehension	list	take apart	judge
	observe	fill in	justify
Application	demonstrate	analyze	criticize
	uncover	take away	solve
Analysis	recognize	put together	decide
	discover	combine	
Synthesis	experiment	imagine	
	organize	suppose	
Evaluation	group	compare	
	collect	contrast	
	apply	add to	
	summarize	predict	
	order	assume	
	classify	translate	
	model	extend	
	construct	hypothesize	

Explanation: These verbs, randomly arranged beside the Taxonomy Model, are representative of the processes exemplified by the model.

APPENDIX III

What Happens to Students When Longer Wait-Times Occur?

1. The length of student responses increases. Explanatory statements increase from 400-800 percent.

2. The number of unsolicited but appropriate responses increases

3. Failure to respond decreases.

4. Confidence of children increases.

5. The incidence of speculative, creative thinking increases.

6. Teacher-centered teaching decreases, and student-centered interaction increases.

7. Students give more evidence before and after inference statements.

8. The number of questions asked by students increases.

9. The number of activities proposed by children increases.

10. Slow students contribute more: From 1.5 to 37 percent.

11. The variety of types of responses increases

12. Discipline problems decrease.

References

Anderson, Thomas. *The Way of the Topi.* Unionville: Royal Fireworks Press, 1996.

Apolozon, Linda Rae. *Stray Cat.* Unionville: Royal Fireworks Press, 1996.

Boeve, Eunice. *Trapped!* Unionville: Royal Fireworks Press, 1997.

Blume, Judy. *Are You There God? It's Me, Margaret.* New York: Bradbury Press, 1970.

Blume, Judy. *Then Again, Maybe I Won't.* New York: Bradbury Press, 1971.

Brown, Joseph. *Dark Things.* Unionville: Royal Fireworks Press, 1995.

Burnford, Sheila. *The Incredible Journey.* Boston: Little, Brown, & Company, 1960.

Byars, Betsy. *The Summer of the Swans.* New York: Viking Press, 1970.

Clemens, Samuel L. *The Adventures of Tom Sawyer.* New York: The Book League of America, 1940.

Dahl, Roald. *Danny, the Champion of the World.* New York: Alfred A. Knopf, 1975.

Deemer, Beth. *The Secret of Poplar Island.* Unionville: Royal Fireworks Press, 1994.

DeClements, Barthe. *6th Grade Can Really Kill You.* New York: Fiking Kestrel, 1985.

Diller, Janelle. *For the Love of Gold.* Unionville: Royal Fireworks Press, 1997.

Farley, Walter. *The Black Stallion.* New York: Random House, 1941.

Fontenay, Charles L. *Kipton & Gruff.* Unionville: Royal Fireworks Press, 1995.

Giff, Patricia Reilly. *Love, From the Fifth Grade Celebrity.* New York: Delacorte Press, 1986.

Greene, Constance C. *A Girl Called Al.* New York: The Viking Press, 1969.

Gunther, John. *Death Be Not Proud, A Memoir.* New York: Harper & Row Publishers, 1949.

Hinton, S. E. *The Outsiders.* New York: The Viking Press, 1967.

Hotaling, Billie. *Count the Stars Through the Cracks.* Unionville: Royal Fireworks Press, 1997.

Kent, Cameron. *Make Me Disappear.* Unionville: Royal Fireworks Press, 1994.

King, Glenda Fountain. *Introducing: Milton S. Tipple.* Unionville: Royal Fireworks Press, 1994.

Konigsburg, E. L. *From the Mixed Up Files of Mrs. Basil E. Frankweiler.* New York: Atheneum, 1967.

Konigsburg, E. L. *Jennifer, Hecate, Macbeth, William McKinley, and Me, Elizabeth.* New York: Atheneum, 1968.

Lawon, Robert. *Ben and Me.* Boston: Little, Brown and Company, 1951.

L'Engle, Madeleine. *A Wrinkle in Time.* New York: Farrar, Straus and Giroux, 1962.

Lewis, C. S. *The Lion, the Witch, and the Wardrobe.* New York: MacMillan Publishing Company, 1950.

London, Jack. *The Call of the Wild.* New York: Platt & Munk, 1960.

Love, Ann. *Taking Control.* Unionville: Royal Fireworks Press, 1997.

Lowry, Lois. *Anastasia, Ask Your Analyst.* Boston: Houston Mifflin Company, 1984.

Mays, Ken. *Harly Weaver and the Race Across America.* Unionville: Royal Fireworks Press, 1994.

Mull, David Kenneth. *The Death of Old Man Hanson.* Unionville: Royal Fireworks Press, 1995.

Paterson, Katherine. *Bridge To Terabithia.* New York: Thomas Y. Crowell Company, 1978.

Pfeffer, Susan Beth. *Kid Power.* New York: Franklin Watts, Inc. 1948.

Piper, Deb. *Jake's the Name, Sixth Grade's the Game.* Unionville: Royal Fireworks Press, 1996.

Raskin, Ellen. *The Westing Game.* New York: E. P. Dutton, 1978.

Rockwell, Thomas. *How To Eat Fried Worms.* New York: Franklin Watts, Inc., 1973.

Rogers, Sherbrooke. *Grandfather Webster's Strange Will.* Unionville: Royal Fireworks Press, 1995.

Saint-Exupery, Antione de. *The Little Prince.* New York: Harcourt, Brace and World, 1943.

Sewell, Ann. *Black Beauty.* New York: Grosset & Dunlap Publishers, 1945.

Siburt, Ruth. *The Dragon Charmer.* Unionville: Royal Fireworks Press, 1996.

Speare, Elizabeth George. *The Sign of the Beaver.* Boston: Houghton Mifflin Company, 1983.

Stamm, Joan. *If I Touched an Eagle.* Unionville: Royal Fireworks Press, 1995.

Steinbeck, John. *The Pearl.* New York: Viking Press, 1953.

Stockton, Frank. *The Lady or the Tiger?* Mankato: Creative Education, 1983.

Taylor, Theodore. *The Cay.* New York: Avon Books, 1969.

Walsh, Lawrence and Suella. *They Would Never Be Friends.* Unionville: Royal Fireworks Press, 1996.

Wells, H. G. *The Inexperienced Ghost.* New York: Funk & Wagnalls, 1970.

Woolf, Paula. *Old Ladies with Brooms Aren't always Witches.* Unionville: Royal Fireworks Press, 1998.